The
UK to USA
DICTIONARY

British English
vs.
American English

By Claudine Dervaes and John Hunter

The
UK to USA
DICTIONARY

British English
vs.
American English

ISBN 978-0-933143-40-1

Library of Congress Control Number: 2011918848

Solitaire Publishing
1090 S. Chateau Pt.
Inverness, FL 34450-3565
(352) 726-5026
www.solitairepublishing.com
e-mail: PSolitaire@aol.com

ABOUT THE AUTHORS

Claudine Dervaes has written and published 14 books for travel education. Her company, Solitaire Publishing Inc., has been in business since 1981. Claudine is a professional speaker and writer. Her "Travel Talk" column appears in the *Ocala Star Banner* and *Gainesville Sun* newspapers (syndicated to the *New York Times*). She teaches a variety of courses at the College of Central Florida. In addition, she works seasonally for Smoky Mountain Jetboats LLC in Bryson City, NC - where she manages the office, captains the jetboats, and leads hikes in the Great Smoky Mountains National Park.

John Hunter, Claudine's husband, is the co-author of **The UK to USA Dictionary.** Born in Scotland, and having lived most of his life in the U.K., he met Claudine in 1987. They married in 1989.

The authors would like to thank the many people who purchased the dictionary in the previous editions and the British specialty stores that carry the books.

Bob's Your Uncle!

*England and America are two countries
separated by a common language.*

Attributed to George Bernard Shaw

TABLE OF CONTENTS

PREFACE

Meanings of some words in this book are obvious. Others can cause confusion/misunderstanding when used in the U.S. or in the U.K. Many Americans find the British terms and expressions amusing and fun and vice versa – which is why this dictionary was written.

Just because slang words are included does not mean the authors condone the use of derogatory expressions. Words generally used throughout Britain and the U.S. have been selected, as opposed to ones that may be used in a certain region or locale. Regional dialects and accents include those of London and the Southeast, Southwest England, the Midlands, West Midlands, East Midlands and Yorkshire, Northwest England, Northeast England, Wales and Scotland. The Welsh language has not been included – it is completely distinct, as is Scottish Gaelic.

It's also important to note that spellings will differ, such as the British vs. American spellings for centre/center, theatre/theater, civilised/civilized, manoeuver/maneuver, etc. The back of the book contains pages of **spelling differences, rhyming slang, pronunciation, cultural specifics, conversion charts, holidays** and **other reference information** about the differences between the U.K. and the U.S. Note: Look for rhyming slang in the comprehensive list at the back rather than in the "dictionary" sections of the book.

We welcome your comments and suggestions.

ABBREVIATIONS USED

abbr.	abbreviation
colloq.	colloquial
dial.	dialect
n.	noun
N. Eng.	Northern England
punc.	punctuation
Sc.	Scottish
v.	verb

USING THIS BOOK

Use this book like any other language dictionary. If you are unfamiliar with a term/expression used in the U.K. – look through the first part of the book.

If it's a U.S. term/expression - use the second part.

Check in the back for rhyming slang, pronunciation, spelling, and many other references regarding the differences between the U.K. and the U.S.A.

UK to USA

BRITISH WORDS/ EXPRESSIONS AND U.S. COUNTERPARTS

UK	USA

A

UK	USA
A BIT OFF	somewhat annoying, unfair
ACCLIMATISED	acclimated
ACID DROP	hard candy with a bitter taste
ADVERT	advertisement/commercial
AERIAL	antenna
AERODROME/PLANE	airdrome/plane
AFTERS	dessert
AGLEY (dialect)	off the intended route/awry
AGONY AUNT	advice columnist
"A" LEVELS	"advanced" high school exams
ALIGHT	disembark
ALUMINIUM	aluminum (note spelling)
ANKLE-BITER	rug rat
ANORAK	parka, also "geek" or "nerd"
ANTI-CLOCKWISE	counter-clockwise
APPROVED SCHOOL	juvenile detention center
ARSE	ass, buttocks
ARTICULATED LORRY	tractor trailer
AS HAPPY AS A SAND BOY	as happy as a lark
AT A PINCH	in a pinch
AUBERGINE	eggplant
AULD LANG SYNE	the old days
AUTUMN	fall

B

UK	USA
BACCY	tobacco
BACK BENCHER	Member of Parliament not a Minister
BACKHANDERS	kickbacks
BACK OF BEYOND	the sticks, the boonies
BAD FORM	bad manners, poor behavior
BADMASH	ruffian
BAFFIES (Sc.)	slippers
BAGS	many, lots
BAGSIE	claim, "dibbs" in U.S.
BAIRN	Scottish child
BAKER-LEGGED	knock-kneed
BAKING TRAY	cookie sheet
BALLS/BALLS-UP	foul-up, messed up
BANGER	sausage
BANGER	firecracker
BANGERS AND MASH	sausages and mashed potatoes
BANG ON	just right, terrific
BANK HOLIDAY	legal holiday
BANK NOTE	bill
BANNED (from driving)	license suspended
BANNOCK (Sc.)	unleavened oatmeal cake
BAP	hamburger bun
BARGEE	person working on a barge

UK	USA
BARM CAKE	hamburger bun
BARMY	crazy/silly
BARNY	fight, argument
BARRISTER	lawyer able to appear in the upper courts
BARTON	farm yard
BASH (HAVE A)	try, attempt
BATMAN	British Army Officer's Orderly
BATHERS	bathing suit
BAWBEE (dialect)	trifle/insignificant thing
BEADLE	church official
BEAK	school headmaster/justice of the peace
BEANO/BEANFEAST	employer's annual dinner/ any celebration dinner
BEASTLY	very unpleasant
BEAVERING	working hard
BED ONLY	hotel room without meals
BEDROOM ENSUITE	room with a private bath
BEDSIDE TABLE	nightstand
BEDSIT/TER	sleeping room (may include kitchen/washroom)
BEER & SKITTLES	pleasure, amusement
BEETLE CRUSHERS	heavy boots
BELISHA BEACON	flashing amber light at a pedestrian crossing

3

UK	USA
BEN (Sc.)	a mountain peak
BERK/BURK	jerk
BESPOKE or MADE TO MEASURE	custom-made
BEST OF BRITISH	good luck
BETTING SHOP	licensed public betting office
BIFFIN	red cooking apple
BIG DIPPER	roller-coaster
BILL (restaurant)	check or tab
BILL (account)	account
BILLY NO-MATES	person without friends
BILLYCOCK (N.Eng)	derby hat
BIN LINER	trash bag
BIRD	woman, "chick" in U.S.
BIRO	ballpoint pen
BIRTHDAY HONOR'S LIST	list of people who have titles given to them on the sovereign's birthday
BISCUIT (sweet)	cookie
BISCUIT	cracker
BIT OF A LAD	a ladies' man
BITS AND BOBS	miscellaneous items
BITTER	popular type of ale
BLACK OR WHITE (coffee)	without or with cream
BLACKLEG/SCAB	scab (strike breaker)
BLACK MARIA	police van
BLACK TREACLE	molasses

4

UK	USA
BLANCMANGE	vanilla pudding
BLAG	"mooch" in U.S.
BLEEDING	similar to "bloody"
BLIGHTER	mean person
BLIMEY (slang)	an oath (from "blind me")
BLIND (window)	shade
BLINDER (TO PLAY A)	to do really well
BLINDING	great
BLINKING	similar to "bloody"
BLOCK OF FLATS	apartment house/building
BLOKE	man or fellow
BLOODY (slang)	expletive, used with other words to mean huge, ex. a "bloody big house"
BLOODY-MINDED	obstinate
BLOOMER	mistake or blooper
BLOOMING (slang)	used like the word bloody
BLOW THE GAFF	give away a secret/plot
BLOWER	phone
BLUE-EYED BOY	fair-haired boy, favorite
BLUE FUNK	state of fright/terror
BOARD	interview, review, or promotion panel
BOB'S YOUR UNCLE	all is well, "you're all set"
BOBBINS	useless junk
BOBBY	police officer
BOBBY-DAZZLER	remarkable, notable person

UK	USA
BODGE	variation of "botch"
BOFF (slang)	copulate
BOFFIN	person engaged in research
BOG	toilet
BOG ROLL	toilet paper roll
BOG STANDARD	basic version, "no frills"
BOGIE	booger, pronounced "bo-gee"
BOILED SWEET	hard candy
BOLLARD	traffic cone, barricade
BOLLOCKING (slang)	"telling-off"
BOLLOCKS (slang)	testicles, "nuts", "rocks" also means "rubbish"
BOMB	a real success
BONCE	person's head
BONK	have sex
BONKERS	crazy
BONNET (auto)	hood
BONNY	pretty, attractive
BOOK	make reservations
BOOK-IN	check-in
BOOK POST	postage for mailing books
BOOK TOKEN	gift certificate redeemable for books
BOOT (auto)	trunk
BOOZER	pub
BORSTAL	juvenile detention center

UK	USA
BOSH	nonsense
BOTHER	expresses impatience
BOTHY (Sc.)	cottage, hut
BOTTLE	nerve
BOTTOM DRAWER	hope chest
BOTTOM GEAR	first gear/lowest gear
BOUGHT A PUP	deceived, swindled
BOWLER	derby hat
BOWLS	lawn bowling
BOX	item protecting a man's genitalia, "cup" in U.S.
BOXING DAY	December 26
BOX ROOM	storeroom (house)
BOX SPANNER	socket wrench
BRACES	suspenders
BRACKETS (punctuation)	parentheses
BRAE (Sc.)	hillside
BRASS FARTHING	a tiny amount, plugged nickel
BRAW (Sc.)	good, fine
BREAD AND BUTTER PUDDING	bread pudding
BREAK	recess at school, work etc.
BREAKER'S YARD	scrap iron dealer, junkyard
BREEZE BLOCK	cinder/cement block
BREW	cup of tea
BRIDGE ROLL	hot dog bun

UK	USA
BRIEF	attorney engaged by a client
BRING AND BUY SALE	swap meet
BRILL	abbreviation for brilliant
BROAD BEAN	lima bean
BROLLY	umbrella
BROTHEL CREEPERS	soft-soled shoes
BROWNED OFF	fed up, bored
BROWN STUDY (IN A)	daydreaming
BUBBLE & SQUEAK	cold meat fried with cabbage and potatoes
BUCKSHEE	something free/a gift
BUGGER (slang)	term of abuse or affection; annoying person, or when affectionately a scamp/rascal
BUGGER ALL (slang)	nothing
BUGGER OFF (slang)	get out of my face, get lost
BUILDING SOCIETY	organization providing loans (especially for house purchases) and investment accounts
BULLRUSH	cattail
BULLY BEEF	corned beef
BUM	buttocks
BUM BAG	fanny pack
BUMF	paperwork/toilet paper
BUNCHES (hair)	pigtails
BUNFIGHT	tea party

UK	USA
BUNGED UP	stopped up
BUNS	muffins/cupcakes
BURGLE	burglarize
BURN (Sc.)	small stream or brook
BUSBY/BEARSKIN	guardsman's tall fur hat
BUSKING	entertaining on the streets for money
BUT AND BEN (Sc.)	two-roomed cottage
BUTTONHOLE	boutonniere
BUTTONS	bellboy
BUTTY, BUTTIES	sandwich, sandwiches
BYRE	cowshed

C

UK	USA
C.V. (Curriculum Vitae)	resume
CABOOSE	ship's galley
CACK-HANDED	clumsy, awkward
CAFÉ	can be pronounced caff"
CAKES AND ALE	the good things of life
CAKE-HOLE (slang)	mouth
CALL BOX	phone booth
CALLOVER (betting)	announcing the latest odds
CAMPER VAN	"RV" in U.S., smaller in U.K.
CANDY FLOSS	cotton candy

UK	USA
CANNON (billiards)	carom
CANTEEN OF CUTLERY	boxed set of cutlery
CAP (sports)	special hat awarded to members of Int'l sports teams
CAPSTAN LATHE	turret lathe
CARAVAN	trailer (recreational)
CARAVANETTE	small R.V. (recreational vehicle)
CAR BOOT SALE	temporary flea market where goods are brought by car and displayed on tables
CAR HIRE	car rental
CAR PARK	parking lot
CAREER (vehicle out of control)	careen
CARETAKER/PORTER	janitor
CAR PARK	parking lot
CARRIAGE PAID	free shipping
CARRIAGEWAY	highway
CARRIER BAG	shopping bag
CARRY ON	continue
CASH POINT	ATM
CASTER SUGAR	white, finely granulated sugar
CASUALTY	emergency room
CATAPULT	slingshot
CATHERINE WHEEL	pinwheel firework

UK	USA
CAT-MINT	catnip
CAT'S EYES	reflectors on roads
CATTLE GRID	Texas gate, cattle guard
CENTRAL RESERVATION	median
CHALK AND CHEESE	meaning "as different as" such as night and day
CHAMPION (N.Eng.)	great; wonderful
CHANCER	risk-taker
CHAP	guy
CHAR (cup of)	tea
CHARABANC	tour bus/motorcoach
CHARLADY	housemaid/cleaning maid
CHARTERED ACCOUNTANT	certified public accountant
CHASE	unenclosed tract of land
CHEAP AND NASTY	low cost and poor quality
CHECKERS (game)	draughts
CHEEK	nerve
CHEEKY	sassy; risque
CHEERIO	goodbye
CHEERS	"thanks" also "goodbye"
CHEESED OFF	exasperated, angry
CHEMIST	pharmacist
CHEMIST SHOP	pharmacy/drugstore
CHEST OF DRAWERS	dresser
CHILD-MINDER	babysitter
CHINWAG	talk, chatter
CHIP BOARD	particleboard

UK	USA
CHIPPY	fish and chips shop
CHIPS	french fries
CHIROPODIST	podiatrist
CHIT	voucher, receipt
CHIVVY	to chase/to hurry up
CHOCK A BLOCK	jammed or crowded
CHOCOLATE/SWEETS	candy
CHORLEY CAKE	small round pastry filled with sultanas
CHRISTMAS CRACKER	wrapped package shaped with twisted ends that two people pull – a snapping noise results
CHUFFED	pleased
CIDER	alcoholic cider/hard cider
CINEMA	movie house/theater
CITY CENTRE	downtown
CITY EDITOR	newspaper editor of business/finance
CLANGER	blunder
CLASS/FORM	(school) grade
CLEARWAY	road where stopping is prohibited
CLERK OF WORKS	construction overseer
CLEVER DICK	know-it-all, smart-alec
CLIPPIE	old term for woman who collects fares on buses, etc.

12

UK	USA
CLOAKROOM	checkroom
CLOAKROOM ATTENDANT	hat/coat check person
CLOBBER	clothing
CLOCK (slang)	hit
CLOTH CAP	blue collar worker
CLOTHES PEG	clothes pin
CLOTTED CREAM	milk thickened by scalding
CLOUGH	narrow valley
COACH	bus
COARSE FISH/ING	fresh water fish/fishing, excluding Salmon and trout
COB	round crisp loaf of bread
COBBLERS	nonsense, bunk
COCK-A-HOOP	elated
COCK A SNOOK	to thumb one's nose
COCK-UP	mistake or blooper
CODLING	a cooking apple
CODSWALLOP	gibberish/nonsense
COCK ABOUT	fool around; mess about
COCKEREL	rooster
COCKNEY	person from London's East End (or thereabouts)
COCK-UP	make a complete mess of
CODSWALLOP	nonsense
COLD COMFORT	little consolation. From Stella Gibbons' book <u>Cold Comfort Farm</u>

UK	USA
COLLAR STIFFENER AND STUD	collar stay and button
COLLECT	pick up or call for
COLLIERY	coal mine with buildings
COMBS (abbreviation for combinations)	combined underwear, long johns
COMMERCIAL TRAVELER	traveling sales rep
COMMISSIONAIRE	uniformed door person at theaters, etc.
COMMUNICATION CORD	emergency handle
COMPERE	show host/master of ceremonies
CONJURER	magician
CONCESSIONS	discounts you might get (students, seniors, repeat customers)
CONKERS	game played with horse chestnuts on strings
CONSCRIPT	draftee
CONSCRIPTION	the draft
CONSTABLE	police officer
CONSTABULARY	police force
COOKER	stove/range
COOKERY BOOK	cookbook
COOK THE BOOKS	falsify records
COPPER (slang)	policeman
COPSE	small wooded area

UK	USA
CORACLE	small wickerwork boat
CORKER	excellent thing
CORN FLOUR	cornstarch
CORNISH PASTY	meat and vegetable turnover
CORPORATION	city government
COSH	blackjack/bludgeon
COS LETTUCE	romaine lettuce
COST A BOMB	to be expensive
COSTERMONGER	street seller of fruits/fish
COT	baby bed/crib
COTTAGE LOAF	loaf of bread made from two pieces, a smaller one on top of a larger one
COTTON BUDS	cotton swabs, "Q-tips"
COTTON REEL	thread spool
COTTON WOOL	cotton balls/cotton pads
COUNCIL HOUSE	the projects; public housing
COURGETTE	zucchini
COURIER	tour escort, tour conductor
COURT SHOES	pumps
COW PAT	cow chip (dung)
COWBOY	dishonest and incompetent tradesman
COWSLIP	marsh marigold
CRANE FLY	daddy-long-legs, harvestman
CREAM CRACKER	soda cracker

UK	USA
CRECHE/NURSERY	day care facility
CRIMBLE/CRIMBO	Christmas
CRISPS	chips (potato)
CROPPER	sudden failure; used in "come a cropper," as in something bad happened
CROWD PULLER	drawing card/draw
CRUMPET	English muffin
CRY OFF	beg off
CRYSTALLISED FRUIT	candied fruit
CUDDY (Sc.)	donkey
CULPABLE HOMICIDE (Sc.)	manslaughter
CULVER	pigeon/dove
CUPBOARD	closet
CUPPA	cup of tea
CUPS (IN ONE'S)	drunk
CURD CHEESE	cottage cheese
CURRENT ACCOUNT	checking account
CUTE	ingenious, clever, attractive
CUT THROAT RAZOR	straight razor
CUTLERY	silverware, flatware

D

UK	USA
DAFT	silly, foolish
DARBIES	handcuffs

UK	USA
DARBY AND JOAN CLUB	club for the elderly
DAVENPORT	writing desk, bureau
DAY TRIPPERS	people on one-day outings
DAYLIGHT ROBBERY	highway robbery
DEAR	expensive
DEASIL (Sc.)	clockwise
DEATH DUTY	inheritance tax
DECOKE (auto)	head/valve job
DEKKO	look
DEMERARA SUGAR	raw brown sugar
DEMISTER	defroster
DEMOB.	military discharge
DEPOSIT ACCOUNT	savings account
DESICCATED (coconut)	shredded
DIAMANTE	rhinestone
DICEY/DODGY	problematic/risky
DICKEY SEAT	rumble seat
DIDDLE	swindle, cheat
DIGESTIVE	round biscuit
DIGS	lodgings
DINNER HOUR	lunch break
DINNER LADY (school)	cafeteria lady
DIP	switch vehicle's lights to low beam
DIRECTORY ENQUIRIES	information
DISORIENTATED	disoriented
DISTRICT	precinct

DIVER (bird)	loon
DIVERSION	detour
DOCH AND DORRIS (WEE) (Sc.)	drink before leaving, one for the road
DOCKET	label listing contents
DODDLE	something very easy
DODGEM	bumper-car
DODGY	cunning; tricky; unreliable
DOG'S BOLLOCKS	something particularly good
DOG'S BREAKFAST/DOG'S DINNER	something which has been made a complete mess
DOG-END	cigarette butt
DOGSBODY	lowly servant
DOING A BOMB	successful
DOLE (THE)	state unemployment benefit
DONE UP LIKE A KIPPER	caught in the act
DONKEY'S YEARS	dog's age
DOSS, DOSS DOWN	lie down
DOSS HOUSE	cheap lodging, flop house
DOUBLE (billiards)	bank shot
DOWNS	hills
DRAPERS	fabric store
DRAUGHT EXCLUDER	weather stripping
DRAUGHTS	checkers, "drafts"
DRAWING PIN	thumbtack

UK	USA
DRESS CIRCLE	mezzanine/loge
DRESSING GOWN	bathrobe
DROP A BRICK	be indiscreet
DROP A CLANGER	make a big mistake
DUCK/DUCK'S EGG (cricket)	out without scoring
DUAL CARRIAGEWAY	divided highway
DUFF	boiled/steamed flour pudding
DUFF GEN	bum steer
DUFF SPARES	bad parts
DUMMY (child's)	pacifier
DUSTBIN	trash can
DUSTCART	garbage truck
DUSTMAN	garbage worker/sanitary engineer
DUSTY (NOT SO)	fairly good
DUTCH CAP	birth control diaphragm

E

UK	USA
EACH WAY BET	win or place
EARTH/EARTHWIRE (electrical)	ground/groundwire
ECCLES CAKE	round pastry cake filled with currants
EGGS AND SOLDIERS	eggs and toast strips

UK	USA
EIDERDOWN	comforter
ELASTOPLAST	band-aid
ELEVENSES	morning coffee/tea break
ELDRITCH (Sc.)	weird, hideous
EMULSION PAINT	flat paint
END OF YOUR TETHER	end of your rope
ENGAGED (phone)	busy
ENGLISH BREAKFAST	cereal, eggs, sausages, bacon, tomatoes, tea, mushrooms, fried bread
ENTREE	meal before the main course
ESQ./ESQUIRE (example: J.Smith, Esq.)	title for a man when Mr. is not used
ESTATE AGENT	realtor
ESTATE CAR SHOOTING BRAKE	station wagon
EX-DIRECTORY	unlisted number
EXTENSION LEAD	extension cord

F

UK	USA
FACE FLANNEL	washcloth
FAFFING AROUND	"pussyfooting" or "bumbling about;" wasting time
FAG	cigarette; tire out

UK	USA
FAGGOT	bundle of sticks; unpleasant woman; homosexual
FAIRY LIGHTS	Christmas lights
FANCY/FANCIED	want or like, wanted or liked
FANCY DRESS	costume
FANNY	vagina
FASH (Sc.)	trouble, bother
FATHER CHRISTMAS	Santa Claus
FED UP	annoyed, frustrated
FEEDER	child's bib/bottle
FELL	mountain, hill, high moorland
FILLING STATION	gas station
FILM	movie
FIRE BRIGADE	fire department
FIRST FLOOR	second floor
FISH MONGER	dealer in fish
FISH SLICE	spatula
FITTED CARPET	wall-to-wall carpet
FIVER	five pound note
FIVES	handball
FIXTURES (sports)	schedule
FLAG DAY	tag day
FLANNEL	nonsense
FLAT	apartment
FLATMATE	roommate
FLAUTIST	flutist

UK	USA
FLEX	electric cord
FLICK KNIFE	switchblade
FLIT (Sc.)	move house
FLOG	sell
FLUID OUNCE (U.K.)	0.9606 U.S. fluid ounces
FLUTTER	small bet
FLY	alert, astute
FLY TIPPING	unauthorized dumping
FLYOVER	overpass
FOOTBALL	soccer
FORCE	small waterfall
FORTNIGHT	two weeks
FRANKING MACHINE	postage meter
FREE HOUSE, FREE OFF LICENCE	pub, liquor store not tied to a brewery
FRIGATE (ship)	small destroyer
FRILLY	lacy
FRINGE (hair)	bangs
FROWSTY	musty, stale smelling
FRUIT MACHINE	slot machine
FUBSY	fat, squat
FULL MARKS	highest grade
FULL MONTY	the whole thing
FULL STOP (punctuation)	period

UK	USA

G

GAFFER	foreman, old man
GAFFER TAPE	duct tape
GALLERY	balcony
GALLON (U.K.)	1.2 U.S. gallons
GAMMON	ham steak
GAMMY (leg)	slightly lame
GAMP	large umbrella
GAMS	legs (usually female)
GANGWAY	aisle
GAOL/GAOLER	jail/jailer
GARDEN	yard
GARTH	paddock, close
GASH	spare, extra
GATEAU	layered cake
GAZUMP	raise the agreed price of a house after receiving a better offer
GEAR LEVER	gear stick, stick shift
GEARBOX	transmission
GEN	information
GEORDIE	person from Newcastle upon Tyne
GET CRACKING	get going
GET KNOTTED	stop annoying me

UK	USA
GET STUCK INTO	eat, enjoy
GET STUFFED	get lost
GET THE HUMP	become irritated, sulk
GET THE PUSH	to be fired, sacked
GEYSER (gas)	water heater
GILL, GHYLL	mountain torrent, ravine
GINGER NUT	ginger snap
GINNEL	narrow alleyway
GIRL GUIDE	Girl Scout
GIVE OVER	stop it
GIVE WAY	yield
GLEN (Sc.)	narrow valley
GLOVE BOX	glove compartment
GOBBET	small amount
GOB (slang)	mouth
GOB STOPPER	jaw breaker
GOBSHITE (Sc.)	bullshit
GOBSMACKED	surprised
GO FOR A BURTON	lost, destroyed, killed
GOODS/GOODS WAGON	freight/freight truck
GOODS LIFT	freight elevator
GOOGLY	curve ball
GOOLIES (slang)	testicles, nuts, rocks
GORBLIMEY/BLIMEY	expression of surprise or indignation
GORMLESS	stupid, lacking sense

UK	USA
GO-SLOW	employees work slower to get employers to improve conditions
GO SPARE	become very annoyed
GRADELY	excellent, handsome
GRAMMAR SCHOOL	high school
GREAT COAT	military overcoat
GREASEPROOF PAPER	waxed paper
GREEN FINGERS	"green thumbs" – someone good with plants
GREENFLY	green aphid, plant louse
GREENGROCER	retailer of fruit and vegetables
GREEN PEPPER	bell pepper
GREET (Sc.)	weep, cry
GRIFF	news, reliable information
GRILL	broil
GRIZZLE	whine, sob
GROTTY	gross, as in disgusting
GROUND FLOOR	first floor
GROUNDAGE	port taxes
GUARD (train)	conductor
GUARD'S VAN (train)	caboose
GUBBINS	gadgets, useless items
GUDGEON PIN	wrist pin
GUINEA	old unit of U.K. currency

UK	USA
GUM	glue or paste
GUY (FAWKES)	effigy of Guy Fawkes burnt on November 5
GYMKHANA	horse riding competition
GYP (GIVE SOMEONE)	torment, treat unmercifully

H

UK	USA
HABERDASHERY	notions store
HAGGIS	Scottish dish made of liver, lung, hearts of sheep boiled in the sheep's stomach
HAIR CLIP	barrette
HAIR GRIP	bobby pin
HAIR SLIDE	barrette
HALF-ROUND	sandwiches made from half slices of bread
HALF-TERM (holiday)	semester/term break
HALT	a way station, whistle-stop
HANDBAG	purse
HANDBRAKE (auto)	emergency brake
HAND LUGGAGE	carry-on baggage
HAND OFF (rugby)	push away opponent with palm of hand
HANGER	wooded area on a steep, sloping hill

UK	USA
HA'P'ORTH (half-penny worth)	slightest, minute quantity
HARD BAKED/BOILED	cynical, disillusioned
HARDCORE	broken bricks and rocks used for road foundations
HARD LINES	bad luck
HARD SHOULDER	emergency lane
HARL (Sc.)	drag along the ground
HASH	the # (pound) symbol
HAVE A GO	give it a try
HAVER	talk foolishly, babble, hesitate
HEADMASTER/MISTRESS	principal
HEATH	open land, covered with low shrubs, usually heather
HEATH ROBINSON	absurdly ingenious and practical; Rube Goldberg
HELTER-SKELTER	corkscrew slide
HEN NIGHT	bachlorette party
HIDE	blind (hunting or observing)
HIGH TEA	evening meal; also a late afternoon meal of tea, sandwiches, scones
HIRE CAR	rental car
HIRE PURCHASE	installment plan
HOARDING	billboard, signboard
HOB	stove top

UK	USA
HOBNAIL BOOTS	jackboots
HOCKEY	field hockey
HOGMANAY (Sc.)	New Year's Eve Celebration
HOKEY COKEY	Hokey pokey
HOLE-IN-THE-WALL	ATM
HOLIDAY	vacation
HOLME	land around river that is subject to flooding
HOMELY (person)	pleasant and unpretentious
HOOTER	horn, siren; also nose
HOOVERING	vacuuming
HOUSING ESTATE	subdivision
HUM	unpleasant smell
HUMBUG	minty, hard-boiled candy
HUNDREDWEIGHT	112 pounds
HUNDREDS AND THOUSANDS	nonpareil

I

UK	USA
ICE CREAM CORNET	ice cream cone
ICED LOLLY	popsicle
ICING SUGAR	powdered/confectioner's sugar
IDENTIFICATION PARADE	line up

UK	USA
IMMERSION HEATER	electric water heater
INCH	small Scottish island
INFANT SCHOOL	school for those age 5-7
INGLE	fire burning in hearth
INGLE NOOK	corner by a fireplace
INJECTION	shot
INLAND REVENUE	internal revenue
INSECT	bug
INTAKE	batch of recruits
INTERIOR SPRUNG	innerspring
INTERVAL	intermission
INVERTED COMMAS	quotation marks
INVIGILATOR	proctor
IRONMONGER	hardware store

J

JAB	shot/inoculation
JACKDAW	small crow
JACKET POTATO	baked potato usually topped with fillings
JANNOCK (dialect)	honest, genuine
JEMMY	jimmy
JERRY	chamber pot
JIGGERY POKERY	underhand scheming
JOBATION	a lengthy reprimand

UK	USA
JOCK	Scottish person
JOE BLOGGS	John Doe
JOINT OF MEAT	roast
JOLLY	very
JOSSER	fellow
JUDDER (mechanical)	vibrate or shake violently
JUG	pitcher
JUGGED HARE	rabbit stew
JUGGERNAUT	very large and heavy truck
JUMBLE SALE	used goods collected and sold, usually for charity
JUMP LEADS	jumper cables
JUMPED QUEUE	cut in line
JUMPER	pullover, sweater
JUNCTION (ROAD)	intersection
JUNIOR SCHOOL	primary school (ages 7-11)

K

KAGOUL	windbreaker; poncho that's usually waterproof
KECKS	trousers
KEEP YOUR PECKER UP	maintain your courage
KEN (Sc.)	know, be acquainted with
KENNEL	dog house
KENSPECKLE	conspicuous

UK	USA
KERB	curb (edge of road)
KERFUFFLE	fuss, commotion
KHAZI	toilet
KICK ONE'S HEELS	to wait around
KILNER JAR	ball/mason jar
KIOSK (phone)	booth
KIOSK (news)	stand
KIP	sleep
KIPPER	smoked herring
KIRBY GRIP	bobby pin
KIRK (Sc.)	church
KISSING GATE	gate allowing people through but not livestock
KIT (sports)	uniform
KIT BAG	soldier's duffel bag
KITCHEN ROLL	paper towel
KITE MARK	official mark indicating goods approved by British Standard Institution
KNACKERED	tired, worn-out
KNACKER'S YARD	place where old horses are slaughtered
KNACKERS (slang)	testicles, nuts, rocks
KNEES UP	lively dance party
KNICKERS	women's panties
KNICKERS IN A TWIST	panties in a wad
KNOCKING SHOP	brothel

UK	USA
KNOCK UP	wake up

L

UK	USA
L PLATE	plate on a vehicle indicating student driver
LABEL	tag
LADDER (hosiery)	run
LADYBIRD	ladybug
LARDER	pantry
LASHINGS	plenty, an abundance
LAST POST	taps
LAY ABOUT	loafer
LAY BY	designated places for vehicles to pull over
LEAD	leash
LEADER/LEADING ARTICLE	main editorial/commentary
LEADER (orchestra)	concertmaster
LEATHERJACKET	harvestman grub
LEFT LUGGAGE	baggage room
LEMON CURD	spread made from eggs, butter, lemons, and sugar
LENDING LIBRARY	public library
LET	lease, rent
LETTER BOX	mailbox

UK	USA
LEVANT	to abscond (debt unpaid)
LEVEL CROSSING	grade/railroad crossing
LIBERTY BOAT	boat carrying sailors ashore on leave
LIBERTY BODICE	closefitting women's undergarment
LICENSED VICTUALLER	innkeeper with a liquor license
LIFT	elevator
LIGHTING UP TIME	time when cars must switch on headlights
LIKE THE CLAPPERS	noisily, with gusto, fast
LIMITED/LTD.	Incorporated/Inc.
LINO	linoleum
LIP SALVE	chapstick
LIQUID PARAFFIN	odorless, tasteless, mild laxative
LIVER SAUSAGE	liverwurst
LOCAL (THE)	tavern, neighborhood pub
LOCH (Sc.)	lake
LOCK UP	shop or garage (without living quarters)
LODGER	boarder
LOLLIPOP LADY/MAN	school crossing guard
LOLLOP	ungainly walk
LOLLY	money
LONG CHALK (BY A)	by a long shot, by far

UK	USA
LOO	bathroom, restroom
LOOSE COVER	slip cover
LOSE ONE'S BOTTLE	"chicken out" in U.S.
LORD MUCK	high-muck-a-muck
LORRY	truck/vehicle carrying large goods
LOSE MARKS	count off
LOUD HAILER	bull horn
LOUNGE SUIT	business suit
LUCERNE	alfalfa/fodder
LUCKY DIP	grab bag
LUG-HOLE (slang)	ear
LUM (Sc.)	chimney
LUNCH BOX (slang)	male genitals under clothing
LUNCHEON VOUCHER	given to employees as part of pay and exchangeable for meals at many restaurants
LURCHER	a cross between a sheepdog and a greyhound
LUTINE BELL	bell rung at Lloyd's of London to announce the loss of a ship

M

MAC, MACK	Mackintosh coat

34

UK	USA
MACARONI-CHEESE	macaroni and cheese
MADEIRA CAKE	rich, sweet sponge cake
MAD ON	crazy about
MAINS	utility lines
MAINS LEAD	outlet plug, adaptor
MAINS RAZOR	electric razor
MAIZE COB	corn on the cob
MAKE A MEAL OF IT	exaggerate
MANKY	gross, as in disgusting
MARCHING ORDERS	walking papers, dismissal
MARKET GARDEN	truck farm
MARMITE	spread made from essence of yeast and beef broth
MARRAM GRASS	dune grass
MARROW (vegetable)	squash
MATCH (soccer)	game
MATE	buddy
MATELOT	sailor
MATHS	math
MAUNDY MONEY	minted silver coins given to the poor by the reigning monarch on Maundy Thursday
MEAN	stingy; cheap
MERCER	dealer in textiles, e.g. silks
MERRY DANCERS	Aurora Borealis
METHS (methylated spirits)	denatured alcohol

UK	USA
MEWS	courtyard stables, often converted into dwellings
MIFFED	upset
MILK FLOAT	light truck (usually electric) for delivering milk
MINCED MEAT/BEEF	hamburger meat, ground beef
MINCER	meat grinder
MIND	watch out for, such as "Mind the step"
"MIND YOUR P'S AND Q'S"	"Be careful to be polite"
MIZZLE	to run away
MOBILE	cell phone
MOCKERS (slang)	curse, misfortune, frustration
MOGGIE	cat
MOIDER/MOITHER	confuse, worry, pester
MOLE GRIP	vise grip
MOKE	donkey
MONEY FOR JAM/OLD ROPE	profit for little effort
MOOR	open land
MORE-ISH	makes you want more
MOT (MINISTRY OF TRANSPORT) TEST	road safety test for vehicles
MOTHER'S DAY	fourth Sunday in Lent

UK	USA
MOTORING	driving
MOTORWAY	freeway
MOVE HOUSE	move
MP	Member of Parliament
MRS. MOP	cleaning woman/housemaid
MUCK IN	get along with
MUCKING ABOUT	messing/horsing around
MUD GUARD	fender
MUG	gullible person
MUGGINS	one who lets him/herself be burdened
MUGS AWAY	the loser starts the next game
MUM	mom; also to keep quiet
MUPPET	dimwit

N

UK	USA
NAAFI	PX
NAFF	rubbish
NAFFED OFF	annoyed, depressed
NAIL VARNISH	nail polish
NANCY/NANCY BOY	effeminate male/homosexual
NANNY	child's nurse
NAPPER	head
NAPPY	diaper

UK	USA
NARK	informer, stool pigeon; also to annoy, make angry
NATIONAL TRUST	conservation organization
NASTY BIT/PIECE OF WORK	contemptible person
NATTER	talk, grumble
NATTY	great; handy
NAVVY	laborer on roads, railway
NEARSIDE (vehicle)	passenger side
NEAR THE KNUCKLE	somewhat indecent
NEAT (drink)	straight
NEB	bill, beak, tip
NEEDLE MATCH	rival match
NEEP (Sc.)	turnip
NET CURTAINS	sheer curtains, under-drapes
NEVER NEVER (THE)	installment plan
NEWMARKET (card game)	Michigan
NEWSAGENT	news dealer/newsstand
NEVER-NEVER	time payment plan
NICK	steal; also condition such as "in good nick"
NICKER	one pound sterling
NIFF	a smell/stink
NIL	no score, zip
999	911
NINETEEN TO THE DOZEN	rapidly, very quickly
NIGGLING	pestering

UK	USA
NIPPER	young boy or girl
NIPPY	agile, nimble, swift
NOB	wealthy or upper class person
NOBBLE	tamper with racehorse to prevent its winning
NOD IS AS GOOD AS A WINK TO A BLIND HORSE	expression about someone who refuses to take a hint
NOD OFF	fall asleep
NOG	strong beer
NOSEY PARKER	overly inquisitive person
NOSH	food (n.)/eat (v.)
NOSH UP	feast, large meal
NOT A FULL SHILLING	mentally deficient
NOT BATTING ON A FULL WICKET	odd, eccentric, insane
NOT HALF	very much
NOT ON YOUR NELLY	no way/certainly not "not on your life"
NOTICE BOARD	bulletin board
NOUGHT	zero, pronounced "nawt"
NOUGHTS & CROSSES	tic-tac-toe
NOWT (N.Eng.)	nothing
NUMBER PLATE	license plate
NURSING HOME	private hospital
NUTTER	crazy person

UK	USA

O

"O" LEVELS	"ordinary" high school exams
OAP (Old Age Pensioner)	senior citizen
ODDS AND SODS	miscellaneous people/things
OFF COLOUR	feeling ill
OFF CUT	remnant
OFF LICENCE	liquor store
OFF PUTTING	disconcerting, repellent
OFF SIDE (vehicle)	driver's side
OFF THE PEG	off the rack
OFF THE RAILS	acting strangely or irresponsibly
OI	"hey" (pronounced "oy")
OLD BILL	police
OLD BOY	alumnus
OLD LAG	hardened criminal
OLD SCHOOL TIE	upper class solidarity
OLD SWEAT	experienced person, old soldier
O.N.O (OR NEAR OFFER)	O.B.O. (or best offer)
ON THE DOLE	receiving unemployment benefits
ON THE MIKE	idling, being lazy

UK	USA
ON YOUR BIKE	exclamation meaning "go away"
ONE-OFF	something that only happens once
OPERATING THEATRE	operating room
OPPO	friend, colleague
OPPOSITION (THE)	main parliamentary party not in office
OPTIC	measuring device attached to liquor/wine bottle necks
ORANGE SQUASH	orange drink
ORBITAL	beltway
ORRA (Sc.)	extra, odd
OUTSIDE BROADCAST	broadcast on location
OVEN CLOTH/GLOVES	potholders/gloves
OVERDRESS	jumper
OVERTAKE	pass
O.V.N.O.	Or Very Near Offer
OWT (N.Eng.)	anything
OXTER (Sc.)	armpit

P

P.A.Y.E. (PAY AS YOU EARN)	income tax deducted from salary

UK	USA
PACK (of cards)	deck
PACK UP	stop working, break down
PADDY	tantrum, fit
PANDA CAR	police patrol car
PANTECHNICON	furniture removal van
PANTOMIME (PANTO)	Christmas show with singing, dancing, slapstick comedy, with audience participation, normally adapted from fairy tales.
PANTS/UNDERPANTS	men's underwear
PARAFFIN	kerosene
PARALYTIC	very drunk
PARCEL	package
PARKY	chilly (weather)
PASS OUT (military)	finish training
PASTY	crusted pie
PATCH (GOOD OR BAD)	period, stage
PATIENCE (card game)	solitaire
PAVEMENT	sidewalk
PAWKY (Sc.)	shrewd, having a dry humor
PAY PACKET	pay envelope
PEAR-SHAPED	gone wrong
PECKISH	slightly hungry
PECULIAR	unique
PELICAN CROSSING	lighted pedestrian crossing
PELMET	valance

42

UK	USA
PENNY DREADFUL	cheap storybook or magazine
PENSIONER	senior
PEPPER POT	pepper shaker
PERMANENT WAY	rail or tram tracks
PERRY	hard cider made from pears
PERSPEX®	plexiglass
PERCY (slang)	penis
PETROL	gasoline, gas
PETROL BOMB	Molotov cocktail
PICTURES	movies
PIGEON PAIR	boy and girl twins
PIG'S EAR	mess, failure
PILLAR BOX	mailbox, mail drop
PILLOCK	stupid person
PINAFORE	apron
PINK	young salmon
PINNY	apron
PINT	20 ounces in U.K. (16 in U.S.)
PIP (THE)	depressed, annoyed
PIPPED AT THE POST	just beaten (in a race)
PIPS	seeds, pits
PISSED	drunk
PITCH (sports)	field
PLANT (billiards)	combination shot
PLASTER	band-aid

UK	USA
PLASTICINE	modeling clay
PLAY GOOSEBERRY	be the extra person, odd one out
PLIMSOLLS/PUMPS	canvas sports shoes, Keds®
PLONKER	idiot
PLOUGHMAN'S LUNCH	meal of bread, cheese, etc.
PLUS-FOURS/TWOS	knickers/knickerbockers
PO-FACED	solemn, humorless
POINT DUTY	traffic duty
POINT PERCY AT THE PORCELAIN	urinate (specific to males)
POLICE INSPECTOR	police captain
POLONECK (sweater)	turtleneck
POLONY	bologna
POLYSTYRENE	Styrofoam
POLYTHENE	polyethylene (such as plastic bags)
POMFRET/PONTEFRACT CAKE	small, flat, round licorice candy
PONCE	pimp; move effeminately
PONTOON (cards)	blackjack, 21
PONY	twenty-five pounds sterling
POOFTER	male homosexual, effeminate man
POP	hock, pawn
POP ONE'S CLOGS	to die

UK	USA
POP ROUND	come to visit
POPPET	small dainty person, term of endearment
PORKIES	from rhyming slang "pork pies" means lies
POSH	upper class. Originates from "port out, starboard home."
POSITIVE DISCRIMINATION	affirmative action
POST	mail
POSTAGE	shipping
POST CODE/POSTAL CODE	zip code
POSTAL ORDER	money order
POSY	small bunch of flowers
POT HOLER	spelunker, cave explorer
POTPLANT	plant in a pot (not marijuana)
POTTED MEAT	head cheese
POTTY	silly, slightly crazy
POWER POINT	electrical outlet
POXY	third-rate, crappy
PRAM (PERAMBULATOR)	baby carriage
PRANG	crash (vehicle)
PRANNET	idiot, fool
PRAWN	shrimp
PREFECT (school)	student monitor

UK	USA
PREGGARS	corruption of the word pregnant
PREP	school homework
PRESENTER	anchorperson
PRESS MARK (library)	call number
PRESS STUDS/POPPERS	snaps
PRIVATE PATIENT	patient not under the National Health Service
PRIVY PURSE	the monarchy's allowance
PROM	concert
PROPER DO (A)	first class social event
PUBLICAN	manager/owner of a tavern
PUBLIC CONVENIENCE	public restroom/toilets
PUBLIC SCHOOL	private school
PUDDING	dessert
PUKKA	the genuine article
PUNCH UP	fight or brawl
PUNCTURE	flat tire
PUNNET	small basket for fruit
PUNTER	customer, specifically of a prostitute; also a gambler
PURCHASE TAX	sales tax
PURLER	fall head first
PURPLE PATCH	good period or spell
PURSE	change purse, coin purse
PUSH CHAIR	stroller
PUT A SOCK IN IT	shut up, be quiet

46

UK	USA
PUT PAID TO	put an end to
PUTTY MEDAL	fit reward for small service

Q

QUARENDEN	red apple
QUARTER DAYS	Mar. 25, Jun. 24, Sep. 29, and Dec. 25
QUARTER-LIGHT (vehicle)	wing window
QUAVER	an eighth note
QUAY	place where boats are loaded and unloaded; pronounced "key"
QUEER ONE'S PITCH	upset one's plans
QUEUE	a line
QUEUE UP	stand in line
QUEUE JUMP	cut in line
QUID	one pound sterling
QUIDS IN	made a profit
QUIFF	curl of hair on forehead

R

RACHMANISM	landlord's exploitation of slum tenants

UK	USA
RAG	prank
RAG AND BONE MAN	itinerant dealer in old clothes and other goods, junkman
RAG DAY/WEEK	annual comic day/week held by students to raise money for charity
RAMP	swindle, usually by overcharging
RANDY	horny
RASHER (bacon)	slice
RATES	property taxes
RATING	non-commissioned sailor
RAWLPLUGS	anchors
RECORDED DELIVERY	certified mail, return receipt
RED CAP	military policeman
REDUNDANT (MADE)	laid off work, riffed
REGISTRY OFFICE	local government office that conducts marriages
REMEMBRANCE DAY	Veteran's Day
REMAND CENTRE	detention center
RETURN (ticket)	round trip
RETURNING OFFICER	official who announces election results
REVERSE CHARGES	call collect
REVERSING LIGHTS	backing up lights, tail lights
RHINE	a large open ditch

UK	USA
RHINO	money, cash
RICK (neck or back)	sprain, twist
RING, RING UP	call
RING ROAD	belt highway
ROCKET	reprimand
ROGER (slang)	have sexual intercourse
ROLLER BLIND	window shade
RORTY	enjoyable
ROTA	roster
ROTOVATOR	power driven soil tiller
ROUNDABOUT	traffic circle; also a merry-go-round
ROUNDERS	game similar to baseball
ROUND TRIP	circular journey
ROUP	sell at auction
ROW	argument, pronounced like "cow" with an "r"
ROWAN TREE	mountain ash
ROYAL MAIL	U.S. Postal Service
RUBBER	eraser
RUBBISH TIP	trash dump
RUCKSACK	backpack
RUDDY	bloody, damned
RUGGER	rugby
RUM (person)	odd, strange
RUNDALE/RUNRIG	joint occupation of land
RUNNER BEAN	string bean

UK	USA
RUNNING KNOT	slipknot
RUN TO	afford
RUN UP	prelude

S

SAFE AS HOUSES	something assured, secure
SAIL CLOSE TO THE WIND	almost get into trouble
SALAD CREAM	like Miracle Whip® - mayonnaise and vinegar
SALOON CAR	sedan
SALT CELLAR	saltshaker
SAND MARTIN	bank swallow
SANITARY TOWEL	sanitary napkin/pad
SAPPER	soldier with the Royal Engineers
SARNIE	sandwich
SASSENACH	Scot's term for English person
SAUSAGE ROLL	sausage meat wrapped in flaky pastry
SAVOURY	non-dessert food
SCAREDY CAT	fraidy cat
SCARPER	to run away
SCATTY	harebrained

UK	USA
SCHTUM	"keep schtum" means keep silent
SCONE	cross between a biscuit and cake, pronounced "skown"
SCOTCH EGG	hard-boiled egg covered in sausage meat and breadcrumbs
SCOUSER	native of Liverpool or the Liverpudlian dialect
SCRAMBLES (motorcycle)	motor cross
SCRIMSHANK	to shirk duty
SCRUB ROUND	avoid or disregard
SCRUMMY	delicious
SCUNNER	to feel sick; a strong dislike
SCUPPER	sink a ship, spoil plans
SECATEURS	pruning shears/clippers
SELLOTAPE	Scotch tape
SEMIBREVE	whole note
SEMI-DETACHED	duplex
SEMIQUAVER	sixteenth note
SEMOLINA	cream of wheat
SEND UP	satirize, ridicule
SERVIETTE	table napkin
SETTEE	loveseat
SHAG (slang)	copulate
SHANDY	an alcoholic mix of lager and British lemonade

UK	USA
SHAW	small wood, thicket
SHIELING (Sc.)	hut used by shepherds/ sportsmen
SHIPPON	cattle shed
SHIRT-LIFTER (slang)	homosexual man
SHOOTING BRAKE	station wagon
SHOOT THE MOON	move house at night to avoid paying rent
SHOPPING PRECINCT	shopping mall
SHORT	cocktail
SHORT A SHINGLE	feeble-minded
SHORT LIST	list of final choices
SHOWER	contemptible/unpleasant person(s)
SHUFTI	a look (at a thing)
SIDEBOARDS	sideburns
SIGNAL BOX (rail)	signal tower
SIGN POST	street sign
SILENCER (auto)	muffler
SILLER (Sc.)	money
SILLY BUGGER	foolish person
SILLY COW	foolish woman
SILVER PAPER	aluminum foil
SILVER SIDE	cut of beef
SIMNEL CAKE	rich fruit cake
SINGLE	one-way ticket
SINGLET	sleeveless undershirt

UK	USA
SISTER (WARD)	senior nurse
SIXPENCE SHORT OF A SHILLING	eccentric, crazy
SKANKY	disgusting
SKELP	hit, beat, spank
SKID CHAINS	snow chains
SKILLY	thin soup
SKIP	dumpster
SKIRTING BOARD	baseboard
SKIVE	avoid work
SKIVVY	a female domestic servant
SLAGGING OFF	picking on
SLAP & TICKLE	boisterous, amorous amusement
SLAPHEAD	bald person
SLASH (slang)	urinate
SLATE	criticize severely
SLEEPERS	railroad ties
SLEEPING PARTNER	silent partner
SLEEPING POLICEMEN	speed bumps
SLIP ROAD	ramp
SLOSH	to hit
SLOSHED	drunk, smashed
SMALLS	underwear
SMASHING	first rate, excellent
SNAFFLE	to steal
SNECK	door latch

UK	USA
SNIGGER	snicker
SNOGGING	making out
SOD (slang)	bastard; short for sodomy
SOD-ALL	nothing
SOD OFF (slang)	go away
SOLICITOR	lawyer, attorney
SONSY (Sc.)	cheerful; buxom
SORT	mend
SPANNER	wrench
SPARE	mad; at one's wits end
SPECIAL CONSTABLE	part-time policeman
SPEECH DAY	annual prize giving day
SPEND A PENNY	go to the toilet
SPINNEY	small wood
SPIV	con man
SPONGE BAG	toiletries bag
SPOT	zit
SPOT ON	right on
SPOTTED DICK	plum duff (see duff) A sponge cake with raisins in it.
SPROG	small child
SQUADDY	private soldier, recruit
SQUEAKY BUM TIME	tense final stages of a competition
SQUIFFY	slightly drunk
STAG NIGHT	bachelor party

UK	USA
STALLS	orchestra seats
STANDARD LAMP	floor lamp
STANDING ORDER	direct/preauthorized debit
STANNARY	tin mine
STARKERS	completely naked
STARTERS	appetizers
STEADY ON	"whoa" in U.S.
STEPS	ladder
STERLING	good; great
STICKY BUN	sweet roll with frosting
STICKY WICKET	sticky situation
STODGY	reluctant to change
STONE (weight)	fourteen pounds
STONES	pits, seeds
STONKING	great
STOP AT HOME	stay at home
STRAIGHT AWAY	right now
STRATH (Sc.)	wide valley
STROLLER	pushchair
STROPPY	bad tempered, awkward
STUMER	worthless money, fraud
STUMP UP	pay up
SUBTOPIA	urban sprawl
SUBWAY	underground pedestrian walkway
SULTANAS	golden raisins
SUMP (auto)	oil pan

UK	USA
SUN BLIND	window awning
SUN CREAM	sunscreen
SUNNIES	sunglasses
SURGERY (doctor's)	office (doctor's or dentist's)
SURGICAL SPIRITS	rubbing alcohol
SUSS OUT	figure out; check over
SUSSED	figured out
SUSPENDERS	garters
SUSPENDER BELT	garter belt
SWALLOW DIVE	swan dive
SWEDE	rutabaga
SWEET	dessert; a candy
SWEET SHOP	candy store
SWINE FEVER	hog cholera
SWINGS AND ROUNDABOUTS	break even; "six of one, half a dozen of the other"
SWING THE LEAD	malinger
SWIPES	inferior beer
SWIMBO	wife or girlfriend, stands for "She who must be obeyed"
SWIMMING COSTUME	bathing suit
SWISS ROLL	jellyroll
SWITCHBACK	roller coaster; road with alternating ups and downs
SWIZZ	to cheat, swindle
SWOT	study in depth for exams

T

TA	thank you
TABLE	submit for discussion, propose
TACKLE	male genitalia
TAIL BACK (traffic)	back up
TAKE A FANCY TO	take a liking to
TAKE-AWAY	take-out
TAKING THE PISS	poking fun
TANNOY	public address system
TAP	faucet
TARMAC	blacktop
TARTAN	plaid
TARTED UP	dressed up
TATTOO	outdoor military display or march
TATTY	shabby
TAXI RANK	taxi stand
TEA	evening meal
TEA CAKE	sweet bun with raisins
TEA TOWEL	dishtowel, kitchen towel
TEDDY BOY	a youth preferring the Edwardian style of dress (a 1950's fad)
TELLY	television

UK	USA
TEN-A-PENNY	dime a dozen
TENNER	ten-pound note
TENPINS	bowling
TENTER	person who looks after things; watchdog
TERRACE HOUSES	row houses
TETCHY	irritable; touchy
THWAITE	some wild land made arable
TICK	credit; also a moment
TICK	a check mark
TICKETY BOO	all right, hunky dory
TICK OVER (vehicle)	idling speed
TICK TACK	manual signaling used by racecourse bookmakers
TIED COTTAGE	occupied by tenant only while working for the owner
TIED HOUSE	pub only allowed to sell a particular brewer's liquor
TIGHTS	panty hose
TILL	cash register
TIME TABLE	schedule
TIP	messy
TIP LORRY	dump truck
TITCH	small person
TITFER	hat
TOAD IN THE HOLE	sausages in Yorkshire pudding

UK	USA
TOE-RAG	tramp, scumbag
TOFF	upper class man, a dandy
TOFFEE NOSED	snobbish, pretentious
TOMATO SAUCE	ketchup
TOMMY	a British soldier
TON	speed of 100 mph; score of 100
TOO CLEVER BY HALF	too smart for his own good
TOODLE-PIP	"goodbye"
TOP DRAWER	of the highest social position
TOP HOLE	first rate
TOPPING	excellent
TOP UP (drink)	refill
TORCH	flashlight
TOT	jigger
TOTTER	junkman
TOWPATH	path alongside a river/canal
TRACKSUIT	sweatsuit
TRAFFIC WARDEN	parking meter patrol person, sometimes assists police in traffic duty
TRAILER (film)	preview (movie)
TRAINERS	sneakers
TRAINSPOTTER	person whose hobby is to spot trains
TRAM	streetcar
TRANSPORT CAFE	truck stop

UK	USA
TRAVELLING RUG	lap robe, lap blanket
TREACLE (BLACK)	molasses
TRIFLE	sponge cake with fruit, wine, jello, custard, cream
TRILBY	fedora
TRIPPER	day vacationer
TROLLEY	shopping cart
TRUG	shallow, wooden garden basket
TRUNCHEON	night stick
TRUNK ROAD	main highway
TUBE	subway
TUCK IN	eat heartily
TUCK SHOP	candy store (usually at a school)
TUPPENNY HA'PENNY	unimportant, worthless, two bit
TURF ACCOUNTANT	bookie
TURN UPS	pant cuffs
TWEE	dainty, quaint
TWICER	double dealer, cheat
TWIG	catch on
TWIT	jerk
TYKE	Yorkshireman; a rascal
TYRE	tire

_UK_	_USA_

U

UNDERGROUND	subway
UNDERLAY	carpet pad
UNIFORM	kit
UNIT TRUST	Municipal Investment Trust
UP THE DUFF (slang)	pregnant
UPPER CIRCLE	first balcony

V

VACUUM FLASK	Thermos
VERGER	church official
VEST	undershirt
VET	to examine and check for accuracy or suitability
VICAR	pastor

W

W.C.	toilet
WAD	sandwich
WAFFLE	to speak or write imprecisely
WAG	to be truant, to play hooky
WAISTCOAT	vest

UK	USA
WALTZER (ride)	tilt a whirl
WANKER (slang)	obnoxious male
WARDER	prison guard
WASH UP	clean dishes, etc.
WASHING-UP POWDER	detergent
WATERBOATMAN	waterbug
WEE (Sc.)	small
WELLIES	waterproof boots
WELLY (auto)	give it some gas
WELSH DRESSER	hutch
WENDY HOUSE	child's playhouse
WHACKED	tired out
WHACKING	huge
WHINGE	whine
WHIP ROUND	collection of money from a group of people
WHITE COFFEE	coffee with cream
WIDE BOY	quick witted but dishonest person
WIFE-BEATER	high alcohol content beer
WILLIE	penis
WINCEYETTE	lightweight flannelette
WINCH (Sc.)	to court or date
WIND CHEATER	windbreaker
WINDLESTRAW	old dry grass
WINDSCREEN	windshield
WIND YOU UP	tease

UK	USA
WINE GUM	gumdrop
WING MIRRORS	side mirrors
WINKLE-PICKERS	long, very pointed shoes
WITTER ON	speak at length about trivial matters
WOBBLER	fit of anger/nerves/panic
WODGE	bunch, clump, chunk
WOOLLY	ill-defined
WONKY	shaky, unreliable
WOTCHER?	how are you?
WREN (Women's Navy)	WAVE
WRITE OFF (vehicle)	to completely wreck, total
WYND (Sc.)	alley, narrow street

Y

UK	USA
Y FRONTS	briefs
YANK	American
YANKEE (betting)	bet on four or more horses to win or place in different races
YOB	lout, hooligan
YONKS	very long time
YORKSHIRE PUDDING	popover-type biscuit
YOU LOT	you guys

UK	USA

Z

ZEBRA CROSSING	pedestrian crossing
ZED	Z
ZIMMER/ZIMMER FRAME	walker
ZIP-FASTENER	zipper

USA to UK

AMERICAN WORDS AND EXPRESSIONS AND BRITISH COUNTERPARTS

USA	UK

A

A LA MODE	served with ice cream
ABSORBENT COTTON	cotton wool
ACCLIMATED	acclimatised
AFFIRMATIVE ACTION	positive discrimination
AIRDROME/PLANE	aerodrome/plane
ALUMNI/AE	former pupils (male/female)
ALUMINUM	aluminium
AMBULANCE CHASER	lawyer who encourages clients to sue for damages after an accident
ANCHORS	rawlplugs
ANTENNA	aerial
APARTMENT	flat
APARTMENT BUILDING	block of flats
APPETIZER	starter
APRON	pinafore/"pinny"
ARROYO	stream, gully
ASHCAN	dustbin
ASS	backside, arse, bum

B

BABYSITTER	child-minder
BACKHOE	mechanical digger
BAD MANNERS	bad form

USA	UK
BAKED POTATO	jacket potato
BALL JAR	Kilner jar
BALLPARK	baseball ground
BALLPARK FIGURE	estimate, approximate amount
BAND-AID	elastoplast
BANGS	hair fringe
BANG UP	first class, terrific
BANK SHOT (billiards)	double
BARF	vomit
BARKEEP	bar tender
BARRETTE	hair clip
BASEBOARD	skirting board
BATHING SUIT	bathers/swimming costume
BAZOO	mouth
BEAN COUNTER	accountant
BEAR CLAW	kind of sweet pastry
BEDROOM COMMUNITY	commuter town/suburb
BELLHOP/BELLPERSON	hotel porter
BELL PEPPER	green pepper
BELLY UP	business failure, shut down
BELT HIGHWAY	ring road
BENNY	overcoat
BILK	swindle
BILL	banknote
BILLBOARD	hoarding
BILLFOLD	wallet

USA	UK
BISCUIT	a soft unsweetened roll
BITCH (slang)	complain
BITCHIN'	great
BITTERSWEET CHOCOLATE	plain chocolate
BLACKJACK	cosh
BLEACHERS	grandstand seats, usually unsheltered
BLIND	hide (observation)
BLINKER	indicator
BLOOPER	blunder, usually in public
BLOWS (it blows)	it's bad
BLUE LAWS	Sunday trading laws
BOARDWALK	raised walkway, usually by the beach
BOBBY PIN	hair grip, kirby grip
BOLOGNA	polony
BOMB	a failure, disaster
BONE UP	to study
BONER	silly idea, blooper, error
BONER (slang)	erection
BOOKMOBILE	mobile library
BOONDOCKS/BOONIES	isolated countryside
BOONDOGGLE	trivial or unnecessary work
BOOTY	bottom, buttocks
BOXCAR (rail)	enclosed goods wagon
BRIEFS	men's underpants
BROIL	grill

USA	UK
BRONX CHEER	blow a raspberry
BUDDY	mate
BUG	insect
BULL HORN	loud hailer
BULL PEN	baseball pitcher's practice area
BUMMER	unpleasant experience
BUNCO/BUNKO	swindle
BUNK	nonsense
BUNS/BUTT (slang)	bum, buttocks
BURGLARIZE	burgle
BURRO	small donkey
BUSBOY/BUSPERSON	waiter's assistant
BUSINESS SUIT	lounge suit
BUSS	kiss
BUSY (phone)	engaged (line)
BUTTE	solitary hill or mountain
BUTTONWOOD/SYCAMORE	plane tree

C

USA	UK
CABANA	beach shelter
CABOOSE (rail)	guard's van
CALABOOSE	prison
CALL (phone)	ring
CALL COLLECT	reverse charges
CALL NUMBER (library)	press mark

USA	UK
CANDIED FRUIT	crystallized fruit
CANDY	sweets, chocolate
CANDY APPLE	toffee apple
CANDY STORE	sweet shop
CAREEN	career
CAR HOP	waiter at a drive-in restaurant
CARNIVAL	fun fair
CARRY-OUT	take away
CART	trolley
CATERCORNER/ CATTYCORNER	diagonally opposite
CATNIP	cat-mint
CATTAIL	bullrush
CERTIFIED MAIL	recorded delivery
CHANGE/COIN PURSE	purse
CHAPSTICK®	lip salve/lip balm
CHARGE ACCOUNT	credit account
CHARLEY HORSE	cramps (arms, legs)
CHECK (mark)	tick
CHECK (payment)	cheque
CHECK (restaurant)	bill
CHECK-IN	book-in
CHECKERS	draughts ("drafts")
CHECKROOM	cloakroom
CHICKADEE	titmouse
CHINCHBUG	destructive lawn insect

USA	UK
CHIPPER	cheerful
CHIPS (potato)	crisps
CHOWDER	fish stew or soup
CINDER BLOCK	breeze block
CITY EDITOR	editor dealing with local news
CITY GOVERNMENT	corporation
CLOSET	cupboard
CLOSET (clothes)	wardrobe
CLOTHESPIN	clothes-peg
COFFEE WITH CREAM	white coffee
COLD COCK	hit hard
COLLAR, STAY AND BUTTON	collar, stiffener and stud
COMBINATION SHOT (billiards)	plant
COMFORTER	eiderdown
COMMERCIALS	adverts
CONDOM	French letter, Durex®
CONDOMINIUM/CONDO	privately owned/leased flat
CONDUCTOR (rail)	guard
CONFECTIONER'S SUGAR	icing sugar
CONNECT (phone)	put through
CONNIPTION (fit)	a fit of rage or hysteria, "throw a wobbler"
CONSTRUCTION	road works

USA	UK
COOKIE	biscuit (sweet)
COOKIE SHEET	baking tray
COOKOUT	barbeque
CORNSTARCH	corn flour
COT	camp bed
COTTAGE CHEESE	curd cheese
COTTON BALL	cotton wool
COTTON CANDY	candy floss
COUCH POTATO	T.V. addict, inactive person
COUNTER-CLOCKWISE	anti-clockwise
COUNT OFF	lose marks
COVER CHARGE	entrance fee
COVERALLS	overalls
COW CHIP	cow pat
CRACKER	biscuit (unsweetened)
CRACK UP	laugh
CRAPSHOOT	risky and uncertain venture
CRAZY BONE	funny bone
CREAM OF WHEAT	semolina
CREEK	stream
CROSSING GUARD	lollipop lady/man
CROSSWALK	zebra crossing
CRUD	filth
CRULLER	small doughnut/cake
CRY UNCLE	admit defeat
CUFFS (on pants)	turn-ups (on trousers)
CUPBOARD	kitchen cabinet

USA	UK
CURB	kerb
CURVE BALL	googly
CUSTOM-MADE	bespoke, made to measure
CUTE	attractive, quaint
CUT THE MUSTARD	meet required standard
CUTTING IN LINE	queue jumping

D

USA	UK
DANDER	temper
DANDY	good
DAVENPORT	large sofa
DEAD TO RIGHTS	red-handed
DEALERSHIP	car manufacturer's franchise
DECK (cards)	pack
DECK SHOES	boat shoes
DEEP SIX	get rid of
DEFROSTER	demister
DELI	delicatessen shop
DENATURED ALCOHOL	methylated spirits/meths
DERBY HAT	bowler hat
DETOUR	diversion
DIAPER	nappy
DICTY	stylish
DIDDLY-SQUAT	nothing
DIDO	prank, caper
DIME STORE	inexpensive store

USA	UK
DINGBAT	stupid person
DINKY	trifling
DISH TOWEL	tea towel
DISHWASHING LIQUID	washing up liquid
DISORIENTED	disorientated
DITSY	silly, stupid
DIVIDED HIGHWAY	dual carriageway
DOCKET	list of court cases
DOGGIE BAG	container provided by restaurants to take leftovers
DOG'S AGE	donkey's years
DOOHICKEY	small object
DOWNTOWN	town centre, city centre
DRAFT (THE)	conscription
DRAPES	curtains
DRESSER	chest of drawers
DRIVING	motoring
DRUGSTORE	chemist shop
DRUNK	pissed
DRY GOODS STORE	drapery
DRYWALL	plasterboard
DUCK SOUP	easy task, money for jam
DUDED UP	dressed up
DUFF (slang)	buttocks
DUMMY UP	keep quiet
DUMPSTER	skip
DUPLEX	semi-detached property

USA	UK

E

EAT CROW	submit to humiliation
EDITORIAL	leader
EFFICIENCY	self-catering apartment
EGGPLANT	aubergine
ELECTRIC CORD	flex
ELEPHANT EAR	deep-fried dough covered in sugar
ELEVATOR	lift
END OF YOUR ROPE	end of your tether
ENGLISH MUFFIN	type of crumpet
ENTREE	main course of meal
ERASER	rubber
ESTATE TAX	death duties

F

FACULTY	staff
FAG	homosexual
FAIR-HAIRED BOY	blue-eyed boy
FALL	autumn
FANNY	buttocks, bottom
FANNY PACK	bum bag
FAUCET	tap
FEEB	stupid person, idiot
FEISTY	aggressive

USA	UK
FENDER (car)	bumper
FENDER (bike)	mudguard
FIELD HOCKEY	hockey
FINK	nasty person, telltale
FIRECRACKER	banger
FIRST BALCONY	upper circle
FIRST FLOOR	ground floor
FIXING TO	preparing to
FIXINGS	meal accompaniments
FLACK	publicity agent
FLASHLIGHT	torch
FLAT PAINT	emulsion
FLATWARE	cutlery
FLIVVER	cheap car or aeroplane
FLOOR LAMP	standard lamp
FLOP HOUSE	doss house
FLUB	botch, bungle
FLUBDUB	pretentious nonsense
FLUID OUNCE (U.S.)	1.041 U.K. fluid ounces
FLUNK	fail
FLUTIST	flautist
FLYER	leaflet
FOOSBALL	table soccer
FRAIDY CAT	scaredy cat
FRANKS	short for frankfurters, hot dogs
FREE SHIPPING	carriage paid

USA	UK
FREEWAY	motorway
FREIGHT/FREIGHT TRUCK	goods/goods wagon
FREIGHT ELEVATOR	goods lift
FRENCH FRIES	chips
FRESHMAN	first year undergraduate
FRIGATE	modern warship
FRITZ (ON THE)	out of order
FRONT DESK	reception
FROSTING	icing
FUN FAIR	school or church bazaar
FUNK	strong smell

G

USA	UK
GABFEST	long spell of talking
GAINER (FULL)	somersault
GALLON (U.S.)	0.833 U.K. gallon
GARAGE SALE	house clearance sale
GARBAGE	rubbish
GARBAGE TRUCK/CAN	dustcart/bin
GARTER BELT	suspender belt
GARTERS	suspenders
GAS/GASOLINE	petrol
GAS STATION	petrol/filling station
GEAR/STICK SHIFT	gear lever
GET ON THE STICK	take hold of the situation

USA	UK
GIVE UP	give over
GIZMO	gadget
GOBBLEDYGOOK	gibberish
GOLDBRICK	shirker, lazy person
GOOF OFF	skive
GOOSE EGG (sports)	duck egg, no score
G.O.P.	Grand Old Party (Republican)
GOUGE	swindle, cheat
GRAB BAG	lucky dip
GRADE	class, form, year
GRADE CROSSING	level crossing
GRADE/GRAMMAR SCHOOL	junior school
GRANDSTANDING	playing to the gallery
GREASE MONKEY	mechanic
GREENBACK	U. S. banknote
GRIDIRON	American football/the field
GRINDER	hardworking student, type of sandwich
GRIPSACK	travelling bag/suitcase
GRITS	maize porridge
GROSS	horrible, foul
GROUND/GROUND WIRE	earth/earthwire
GROUND BEEF	minced beef
GRUBSTAKE	expecting a share of profits investment in an enterprise

USA	UK
GULCH	ravine, gully
GUMBO	spicy soup made with okra
GUMSHOE	galosh, detective

H

HABERDASHERY	a men's clothing and furnishings shop
HALF STAFF	half-mast
HAMBURGER BUN	bap
HAMBURGER MEAT	minced beef
HAND OFF (sports)	to hand the ball to a teammate
HAPPENSTANCE	happens by chance
HARD CANDY	boiled sweets
HARDSCRABBLE	minimum return from maximum effort
HARDWARE STORE	ironmongers
HARVESTMAN	daddy longlegs
HASH-SLINGER	waiter/waitress
HATCHECK PERSON	cloakroom attendant
HAUL/HAUL ASS	to go fast
HAVE A GANDER	have a look
HAZING	bullying, humiliating
HEAD	toilet
HEADCHEESE	potted meat
HEAD/VALVE JOB (auto)	decoke

USA	UK
HEATER	handgun/firearm
HEINIE	bum, buttocks
HEIST	robbery
HELLION	mischievous, troublesome
HICK	country bumpkin
HICKEY	love bite, also a pipe bender
HIGH BALL	whiskey and water with ice
HIGHBINDER	swindler or ruffian
HIGH BOY	tall boy
HIGH-MUCK-A-MUCK	Lord muck
HIGH ROLLER	big spender
HIGH TAIL	rush, get out fast
HIKE	raise
HOBO	tramp or wanderer
HOCK/IN HOCK	pawn/in debt
HOCKEY	ice hockey
HOCUS POCUS	jiggery pokery
HOG CHOLERA	swine fever
HOG PEN	pigsty
HOKEY	corny
HOKEY POKEY	hokey cokey (participation dance)
HOMELY (person)	ugly, unattractive
HOMEMAKER	housewife
HOMER	home run in baseball
HOMINY	processed maize, see also grits

USA	UK
HONCHO, HEAD HONCHO	boss
HOOCH	alcoholic drink, usually illicit
HOOD (auto)	bonnet
HOOEY	nonsense
HOOKY (play)	truant
HOOSEGOW	prison
HOOTERS	breasts
HOPE CHEST	bottom drawer
HORNY	randy
HORSE OPERA	western film
HORSING AROUND	mucking about
HOT DOG BUN	bridge roll
HUNDREDWEIGHT	100 pounds
HUNK	attractive man
HUNKY-DORY	fine, satisfactory
HUSH PUPPY	quick-fried maize bread
HUTCH	Welsh dresser

I

ICEBOX	refrigerator
ICE CREAM CONE	ice cream cornet
INCORPORATED/INC.	Limited/Ltd.
INFORMATION (phone)	directory enquiries
INNERSPRING	interior sprung
INSTALLMENT PLAN	hire purchase

USA	UK
INTERMISSION	interval
INTERN	medical graduate
INTERSECTION	road junction
INTIMATE APPAREL	lingerie

J

USA	UK
JACKHAMMER	pneumatic hammer
JACKRABBIT	hare
JAMMIES	pyjamas
JAVA	coffee
JAW BREAKER	gob stopper
JELLO	gelatin dessert, jelly
JELLY ROLL	Swiss roll
JIBE (nautical)	tack
JIBE	agree with, fit in with
JIGGER	tot
JIMMY	jemmy
JITNEY	small bus, jeep
JIVE	tease, fool; meaningless talk
JOCK	athletic male
JOHN	toilet
JOHN DOE	Joe Bloggs
JOHN HENRY/HANCOCK	person's signature
JOHNNY-JUMP-UP	violet/pansy
JOHNSON (slang)	penis
JUMBLE	small circular sweet-cake

USA	UK
JUMP ROPE	skip rope

K

KAFFEE KLATSCH	coffee morning/informal gathering
KEDS	plimsolls
KEGLER	bowler, skittle player
KEISTER	arse
KEROSINE/KEROSENE	paraffin
KLUTZ	awkward, clumsy
KNICKERS	plus fours
KNOCK UP	make pregnant
KOOK	crazy or eccentric person
KUDOS	good show, well done

L

LACY	frilly
LADYBUG	ladybird
LADYFINGER	finger-shaped sponge cake
LAID OFF	made redundant
LALLYGAG	to loiter
LAP ROBE	travelling rug
LAUNDROMAT	laundrette
LAWN BOWLING	green bowling

USA	UK
LEARNER'S PERMIT	provisional driver's licence
LEASE	let
LEASH	lead
LEERY	wary
LEGAL HOLIDAY	bank holiday
LICENSE PLATE	vehicle number plate
LIGHTNING BUG	firefly
LIMA BEAN	broad bean
LIMP WRIST (slang)	nancy boy
LINE (stand in)	queue (up)
LINE UP	identification parade
LIP SYNCH	mime to recorded music
LIQUOR	spirits
LIQUOR STORE	off licence
LIVERWURST	liver sausage
LOADED FOR BEAR	fully prepared
LOAN SHARK	one who charges interest at an unlawful rate
LOBBY	foyer
LOCATE	settle at home/business
LOCATOR	one who determines land boundaries when disputed
LOCOMOTIVE ENGINEER	train driver
LOGE	front dress circle
LOGGER	lumberjack
LOGY	sluggish, lethargic
LONG DOZEN	baker's dozen (13)

85

USA	UK
LONG GREEN	paper money
LOVE SEAT	settee, usually a two-seater
LUMBER ROOM	box room
LUMMOX	clumsy person
LUNCH MEAT	sliced meat for sandwiches
LUSH	an alcoholic

M

USA	UK
MACKINAW	a warm, belted cloth coat
MAKING OUT	snogging
MAIL	post
MAIL CARRIER/MAILMAN	postal carrier/postman
MAIL DROP	pillar box
MAILMAN	postman
MAIN STEM	main street
MAJOR LEAGUE	principal league in professional baseball
MALL (SHOPPING)	precinct/arcade
MANSLAUGHTER	culpable homicide
MARKERS	felt tip pens
MASON JAR	Kilner jar
MASS TRANSIT	public transport
MEAT GRINDER	mincer
MEDIAN	central reservation
MEDICAID	government sponsored medical aid for the needy

USA	UK
MEDICARE	government insurance program providing medical care for the elderly
MELD	to blend, combine, mix
MESA	a high, steep-sided, rocky plateau
MEZZANINE	dress circle
MICHIGAN (card game)	Newmarket
MINOR LEAGUE	other than the principal (major) league in baseball
MOLASSES	black treacle
MONEY ORDER	postal order
MONKEY WRENCH	adjustable spanner
MOOCH	blag
MOONSHINE	illicit liquor
MORTICIAN	undertaker
MOTHER'S DAY	second Sunday in May
MOTORCROSS	scrambles
MOVIE THEATER	cinema
MOVIES	pictures, films
MOVING TRUCK	removal van
MOXIE	courage, daring, energy
MUFFIN	bun
MUFFLER (auto)	silencer
MUGWUMP	one who "sits on the fence"
MULLIGAN	a meat and vegetable stew
MUTUAL FUND	unit trust

N

NAIL POLISH	nail varnish
NAPKIN	serviette
NATATORIUM	indoor swimming pool
NEW YORK MINUTE	quickly
NEWSDEALER/NEWSTAND	newsagent
NEWSHAWK/NEWSHOUND	reporter
NICKELODEON	early jukebox
NIGHTSTICK	truncheon
NIGHT TABLE/NIGHTSTAND	bedside table
911	999
NIPPLE (on baby bottle)	teat
NONPAREIL	hundreds and thousands
NOTARIZE	attest as a notary
NOT HAY	a lot of money
NOTIONS STORE	haberdashery
NUKE IT	cook in a microwave oven

O

OATMEAL	porridge
OFF-COLOR	somewhat indecent
OFFICE (doctor's)	surgery
OFF THE RACK	off the peg
OFF THE WALL	bizarre, strange
OIL PAN	sump

USA	UK
ONE WAY TICKET	single ticket
ON TAP (beer)	draught
ON THE LAM	running away
ON THE NOSE	precisely
ORCHESTRA SEATS	stalls
ORNERY	unpleasant, cantankerous
OUTLET	power point
OUTLET PLUG	mains lead
OUT OF WHACK	out of order
OUT TO LUNCH	crazy
OVERPASS	fly over

P

PACIFIER	dummy
PACKAGE	parcel
PACKAGE STORE	off license
PADDLE (ping pong)	bat (table tennis)
PALOOKA	lout, poor performer at sport
PANHANDLE	to beg in the street
PANHANDLE	narrow projecting strip of land such as in Texas
PANTIES	knickers
PANTIES IN A WAD	knickers in a twist
PANTIHOSE	tights
PANTYWAIST	nancy boy, effeminate man
PAP SMEAR	cervical smear

USA	UK
PAPER ROUTE	paper round
PAPER TOWEL	kitchen towel
PARKING LOT	car park
PARTICLE BOARD	chipboard
PASS (vehicle)	overtake
PASTOR	vicar
PATSY	scapegoat, victimised or deceived person
PAVEMENT	roadway
PAY PHONE	call box, phone booht
PEDESTRIAN CROSSING	zebra crossing
PEEPER	private detective
PENITENTIARY	prison
PENNY-ANTE	petty, insignificant
PEPPER SHAKER	pepper pot
PERIOD (punctuation)	full stop
PHARMACY	chemist
PHI BETA KAPPA	member of the oldest college fraternity
PICKY	fussy, finicky
PINCH HITTER	substitute
PINKSTER	Whitsuntide
PINOCHLE	pronounced "P nuckle" - card game with double pack (9s to aces only)
PINOLE	flour made from parched corn flour

USA	UK
PINTO	piebald horse
PISSED	angry
PIT	stone of a fruit
PITCHER	jug
PITMAN (mechanism)	connecting rod
PLACE BET	horse to be first or second
PLASTIC WRAP	cling film
PLEXIGLASS	Perspex®
PLUGGED NICKEL	brass farthing
PLUG UGLY	ruffian, gangster
PODIATRIST	chiropodist
POLICE CAPTAIN	police inspector
POLLIWOG	tadpole
PONDEROSA	pine tree
PONY CAR	sporty two-door car
POPSICLE	iced lolly
POSTAGE METER	franking machine
POT CHEESE	cottage cheese
POT HOLDERS/GLOVES	oven cloth/gloves
POUND (# symbol)	hash
POWDERED SUGAR	icing sugar
PRAIRIE SCHOONER	large covered wagon
PRECINCT	district
PREVIEW (movies)	trailer
PRINCIPAL	headmaster/headmistress
PRIVATE SCHOOL	public school
PROCTOR	invigilator

USA	UK
PROM	school dance
PUBLIC SCHOOL	school managed by public authorities
PUMP	ladies court shoe
PURSE	handbag
PUSSY-WHIPPED	hen-pecked
PX (post exchange)	NAAFI

Q

QUAHOG	edible clam
QUARTER DAYS	Jan. 1, Apr. 1, Jul. 1, Oct. 1
QUARTER HORSE	horse bred to run strongly over the quarter mile
QUARTER NOTE	crotchet
QUIRT	riding crop
QUONSET HUT	Nissen hut
QUOTATION MARKS	inverted commas

R

RAILROAD TIES	railway sleepers
RAIN CHECK	postponement
RAMP	slip road
RANGE	cooker
RANGER	park/forest warden
RATTLER	goods train; rattlesnake

USA	UK
RAZZ	tease, deride
REALTOR	estate agent
REALTY	real estate
RECAP (tire)	retread
RECEIPT	chit
RECESS (school)	break
REFLECTORS IN THE ROAD	cat's eyes
RESTROOM	toilet/W.C.
RÉSUMÉ	C.V. (Curriculum Vitae)
RHINESTONE	diamante
RHUBARB	expression for a heated dispute
RIFFED	sacked, made redundant
RINKY DINK	old fashioned, dilapidated
ROACH	cockroach
ROBE	dressing gown
ROMAINE LETTUCE	cos lettuce
ROOKIE	new team member
ROOSTER	cockerel
ROOT BEER	soda pop made from plant root extracts
ROUGH RIDER	person who breaks in horses
ROUND TRIP	return
ROUSTABOUT	unskilled labourer
ROWEN	aftermath, field of stubble
ROW HOUSE	terraced house
RUBBING ALCOHOL	surgical spirit

USA	UK
RUBE	yokel
RUBE GOLDBERG	Heath Robinson
RUMBLE	fight
RUMBLE SEAT	dickey seat
RUMPUS ROOM	games room
RUN (stockings)	ladder
RUTABAGA	swede
RV	caravan

S

USA	UK
SAD SACK	very inept person
SALAD DRESSING	varieties of oil, vinegar and/or many other ingredients to go on top a salad
SALES CLERK	shop assistant
SALUTATORIAN	second ranking member of a graduating class who delivers an opening speech at graduation
SAND DOLLAR	round flat sea urchin
SARAN WRAP®	cling film
SASHAY	walk ostentatiously/casually
SASSY	cheeky, saucy
SAW BUCK	ten dollar bill
SCADS	large quantities, lashings

USA	UK
SCALPER	ticket tout
SCAM	rip off
SCHEDULE	timetable
SCHLEMIEL	foolish or unlucky person
SCHLOCH	poor quality; secondhand
SCOPE OUT	check into, investigate
SCOTCH TAPE	Sellotape®
SCRAPPLE	stewed meat and flour pressed into cakes
SCRATCH PAD	scribbling pad
SCREEN	window/door netting, allowing air through, but not insects
SCREWBALL	strange or crazy person
SCROD	last/freshest catch of the day
SCUTTLEBUTT	rumour
SECOND FLOOR	first floor
SECOND GUESS	know by hindsight
SECOND STOREY MAN	cat burglar
SEDAN	family car, saloon car
SEEDS	pips
SEE-SAW	teeter-totter
SELF-RISING FLOUR	self-raising flour
SEMESTER (school)	term
SEND UP	put in prison
SHAKE DOWN	extort money from; a raid
SHARK	outstanding student

USA	UK
SHAVE TAIL	mule just broken in
SHEDDING	moulting
SHEERS	net curtains
SHILL	person used as a decoy
SHIPPING	postage
SHIRT WAIST	blouse
SHOAT	piglet
SHOO FLY	temporary road or railway; guard to watch people
SHOO FLY PIE	sweet treacle dessert
SHOO IN	a certainty
SHOPPING CART	trolley
SHOTS	jabs, inoculations
SHOWER	party to give presents to a prospective bride/expectant mother
SHREDDED (coconut)	desiccated
SHRIMP	prawn
SHUCK	remove shells from oysters, to discard
SHUCKS	an expression meaning something worthless
SIDEBURNS	sideboards
SIDEWALK	pavement
SIDING	building's exterior cladding
SIGNAL TOWER	signal box
SILVERWARE	cutlery

USA	UK
SKID ROW	part of town frequented by vagrants, alcoholics, etc.
SKIN GAME	swindling game, confidence trick
SKIVVIES	underwear
SLATE	schedule; nominate
SLEW	a large number, many
SLICKER	a plausible rogue
SLINGSHOT	catapult
SLIP COVER	loose cover
SLOWPOKE	slowcoach
SMART-ALEC	clever dick
SNAP	easy task
SNAPS	press studs
SNEAKERS	plimsolls/gym shoes/trainers
SNICKER	snigger
SNOLLYGOSTER	shrewd/unscrupulous person
SNOW JOB	attempt to persuade by misleading talk
SNOWED UNDER	overwhelmed
SOCKDOLOGER	decisive blow
SOD	turf
SODA	pop, soda pop
SODA CRACKER	cream cracker
SOLITAIRE (cards)	patience
SOPHOMORE	second year student at high school/Undergraduate

USA	UK
SPATULA	fish slice
SPEED BUMPS	sleeping policemen
SPELUNKER	pot holer
SPIEL	glib or persuasive speech
SQUASH	marrow
STAKE OUT	to place under surveillance
STANDPATTER	opposed to change
STAND THE GAFF	endure hardship
STAND IN LINE	queue up
STATION WAGON	estate car
STAY AT HOME	stop at home
STEAL (A)	a bargain; easy task
STICK SHIFT	gear lever/stick
STOGY	long cigar
STOLE MY THUNDER	said or did something before I could
STOOL PIGEON	copper's nark
STOOP	small porch, staircase at a building's entrance
STOPLIGHT	traffic light
STREETCAR	tram
STREET SIGN	signpost
STRING BEAN	runner bean
STROLLER	push chair
STUDIO APT.	a bedsit
STYROFOAM	polystyrene

USA	UK
SUBDIVISION	housing estate
SUBWAY	tube, underground
SUCKS (slang)	hatred, disgusting
SUCKER	toffy lolly
SURF & TURF	a beef and seafood meal
SUSPENDERS	braces
SWAN DIVE	swallow dive
SWEATER	jumper
SWEATSUIT	tracksuit
SWING SHIFT	night shift
SWITCHBACK	road with alternating left and right bends
SWITCHBLADE	flick knife

T

TAD	small amount, small boy
TAFFY	a kind of toffee
TAG	motor vehicle license plate
TAG DAY	flag day
TAKE A TURN	have a go
TAKE OUT	take away
TALK TURKEY	be straightforward
TAR HEEL	native of North Carolina
TEAMSTER	lorry driver
TEETER-TOTTER	seesaw
TEMBLOR	earthquake

USA	UK
TEXAS GATE	cattle grid
THUMB TACK	drawing pin
TICK-TACK-TOE	noughts and crosses
TIGHTWAD	miserly person
TILT A WHIRL	waltzer
TIRE	tyre
TO GO	take-away
TOTAL (vehicle)	write off
TOUCH BASE	contact, get in touch with
TRACK MEET	track and field competition
TRACTOR TRAILER	articulated lorry
TRAFFIC CIRCLE	roundabout
TRAILER	caravan
TRAILER PARK	caravan site
TRANSMISSION	gear box
TRASH CAN	dustbin
TRAVEL TRAILER	caravan
TRICKY	dodgy
TRUCK FARM	market garden
TRUCK STOP	transport cafe
TRUNK (car)	boot
TUCKERED OUT	tired out, knackered
TURRET LATHE	capstan lathe
TURTLENECK	polo neck
TUXEDO/TUX	dinner jacket
TWO BIT	petty, small time
TWO BITS	25 cents

100

USA	UK
TWO CENTS	an opinion, two pence, tuppence

U

USA	UK
UNDERGRADUATES	
FRESHMAN	1st year
SOPHOMORE	2nd year
JUNIOR, SENIOR	3rd year, 4th year
UNDERSHIRT	singlet
UNLISTED NUMBER	ex-directory
UP CHUCK	vomit
UPSCALE	upmarket
UPTOWN	"downtown" in most cities, often implies an upscale neighborhood
U.S. POSTAL SERVICE	Royal Mail
UTILITY LINES	mains

V

USA	UK
VS. (versus)	V.
VACUUM	hoover
VALANCE	pelmet
VALEDICTORIAN	highest ranking student in a graduating class who gives graduation farewell speech

USA	UK
VEST	waistcoat
VETERAN	ex-serviceman
VETERANS' DAY	Remembrance Day
VOUCHER	chit

W

USA	UK
WALKING PAPERS	marching orders, dismissal
WALL-TO-WALL CARPET	fitted carpet
WASH CLOTH	face flannel
WASH UP	wash hands and face
WASTEBASKET	dustbin
WAVE (Women's navy)	WREN
WAXED PAPER	greaseproof paper
WAY STATION	minor railway station, a halt
WET BACK (vulgar)	illegal immigrant from Mexico
WHAMMY	hex, setback, shocking blow
WHISTLE-STOP	minor railway station, a halt
WHOLE NOTE	semibreve
WICKET	small sliding window or opening (e.g. at a ticket office)
WIND BREAKER	wind cheater
WINDSHIELD	windscreen
WINGDING	wild party
WISEGUY	mobster, know-it-all

USA	UK
WRECKER	breakdown lorry
WRIST PIN	gudgeon pin

Y

USA	UK
YARD	garden of a house
YARD SALE	house clearance sale
YAWP	to cry out; to talk continually and noisily
YEGG	burglar, safecracker
YELLOW DOG	mongrel; someone anti-union
Y'ALL (YOU ALL)	you

Z

USA	UK
Z	Zed
ZILCH	nothing
ZINGER	sharp witticism
ZIP	nil, no score, nothing
ZIP CODE	postal code
ZIP IT	keep mum
ZIT	spot
ZUCCHINI	courgette

NOTES

RHYMING SLANG

Rhyming slang is a type of code supposedly invented by the Cockneys who resented having to work with Irish immigrants. They devised the rhyming words to not be understood. You can pretty much make up your own and the list changes all the time as some go in and out of favor. Sometimes the rhyming part is even omitted! For example: "Have a butcher's" means "Have a look" (from "butcher's hook = look") - What fun!

A la mode	Code
Abraham Lincoln	Stinking
Ace of Spades	AIDS
Acid Trip	Rip
Acker Bilk	Milk
Adam and Eve	Believe
Adam and the Ants	Plants/Pants
Airs and Graces	Faces/Braces
Alan Minter	Splinter/Printer
Almond Rocks	Socks
Alligator	Later
Ancient Greek	Freak/Reek
Andy Cain	Rain
Apples and Pears	Stairs
Apple Fritter	Bitter (beer)
April Showers	Flowers
Army and Navy	Gravy
Arthur Ashe	Cash/Slash
Aunt Mabel	Table
Aunt Nell	Smell
Auntie Nelly	Belly/Telly
Bacon and Eggs	Legs

Bacon Rind	Blind/Mind
Bag for Life	Wife
Bag/Bowl of Fruit	Suit
Bag of Yeast	Priest/Beast
Baked Beans	Jeans
Bamboo Shoots	Boots
Bangers and Mash	Trash/Cash
Barbed Wired	Tired
Barney Rubble	Trouble/Double
Bat and Ball	Tall
Bat and Wicket	Ticket
Bath Tub	Pub
Belt Buckle	Chuckle
Bees and Honey	Money
Bell Ringers	Fingers
Ben Dover	Hangover
Benny Hills	Pills
Bib and Brace	Face
Big Ben	Ten
Big Dippers	Slippers
Bill and Ben	Ten/Pen
Bill Murray	Curry
Billy Bunter	Punter (prostitute's customer)/Gambler
Billy Goat	Throat
Bin Lids	Kids
Bird Bath	Laugh
Bird's Nest	Chest
Biscuit and Cookie	Rookie/Bookie
Biscuits and cheese	Knees
Blood Red	Head

106

Bo Peep	Sleep
Boat Race	Face
Boiler House	Spouse
Bonny Fair	Hair
Bottle Stopper	Copper (policeman)
Box of Toys	Noise
Brady Bunch	Lunch
Bread and Butter	Nutter/Gutter
Bread and Cheese	Sneeze
Bread and Honey	Money
Bread Knife	Wife
Bride and Groom	Living Room
Bride and Groom	Broom
Britney Spears	Tears/Ears/Beers
Brown Bread	Dead
Brown Hat	Cat
Bruce Lee	Key/Tea/Pee
Brussel Sprout	Shout
Bubble and Squeak	Week/Greek
Bubble Bath	Laugh
Bug and Flea	Tea
Bunsen Burner	Earner
Burton-on-Trent	Rent
Butcher's Hook	Look
Cab Rank	Bank
Callard and Bowsers	Trousers
Calvin Klein	Wine
Cane and Abel	Table
Captain Cook	Look/Book
Captain Kirk	Work/Turk
Car and Scooter	Computer

Carving Knife	Wife
Cat and Mouse	House
Chalk Farm	Arm
Cherry Pie	Lie
Chevy Chase	Face
Chicken and Rice	Nice
Chicken Dinner	Winner
Chicken Jalfrezi	Crazy
Chinese Chippy	Nippy
Chip Butty	Nutty
Chips and Peas	Knees
Christmas Crackered	Knackered (tired)
Christmas Eve	Believe
Church Pews	Shoes
Claire Rayners	Trainers (running shoes)
Clark Gable	Table
Clever Mike	Bike
Clothes Peg	Egg
Coat Hanger	Clanger (mistake)
Cock and Hen	Ten
Cock Linnet	Minute (of time)
Cockney Rhyme	Time
Condoleezza Rice	Price
Cooking Fat	Cat
Cornish Pasty	Nasty
Corns and Bunions	Onions
Cough and Sneeze	Cheese
Cow's calf	Laugh
Cream Crackered	Knackered (tired)
Cream Rice	Nice

Currant Bun	Son/Nun/Sun
Dad's Army	Barmy (crazy)
Daisy Roots	Boots
Dancing Bears	Stairs
Dancing Fleas	Keys
Daniel Boone	Spoon
Danny Glover	Lover
Davy Crockett	Pocket
Day Trippers	Slippers
Deep Fat Fryer	Liar
Dick Van Dyke	Bike
Dicky Bird	Word
Didgeridoo	Clue
Diet Coke	Joke
Dig the Grave	Shave
Dinner Plate	Mate
Dickory Dock	Clock
Dicky Dirt	Shirt
Dirty Daughter	Water
Dog and Bone	Phone
Donkey's Ears	Years
Dot and Carried	Married
Dot and Dash	Cash
Drum and Bass	Face/Place
Drum Roll	Hole
Duck and Dive	Hide
Duke of Kent	Rent/Bent
Duke of York	Fork
Dustbin Lid	Kid
Early Hours	Flowers
Easter Bunny	Funny

Egg Yolk	Joke
Eggs and Kippers	Slippers
Eighteen Pence	Sense
Elliott Ness	Mess
Faith and Hope	Soap
Fat Boy Slim	Gym
Fawlty Tower	Shower
Feather and Flip	Kip (sleep)
Field of Wheat	Street
Fish and Chips	Hips
Fish Hook	Book
Flounder and Dab	Cab
Frasier Crane	Pain
Fred Astaire	Chair/Hair
Fred McMurray	Curry
Friar Tuck	Luck
Frog and Toad	Road
Gang and Mob	Gob (mouth)
Garden Fence	Dense
Garden Gate	Mate/Magistrate
Garden Tool	Fool
Gates of Rome	Home
Gay and Frisky	Whisky
George Michael	Cycle
German Beer	Engineer
German Flutes	Boots
Giraffe	Laugh
Glorious Sinner	Dinner
Gold Watch	Scotch
Gregory Peck	Cheque/Neck
Hairy Chest	Very Best

Hairy Knees	Please
Hairy Toes	Nose
Hale and Hearty	Party
Ham and Cheesy	Easy
Ham Shank	Yank
Hank Marvin	Starvin'
Harry and Billy	Silly
Harry Holt	Bolt (run away)
Heavenly Bliss	Kiss
Herring Bone	Phone
Hit or miss	Kiss
Holy Ghost	Toast/Racing Post
Holy Grail	Email
Honey Bees	Keys
Ice Rink	Drink
Inky Smudge	Judge
Insect and Ants	Pants
Irish Jig	Wig
Irish Stew	True
Ivory Band	Hand
J. Arthur Rank	Bank
J. R. Ewing	Viewing
Jack and Jill	Till/Bill/Pill
Jack Jones	On Your Own
Jackie Chan	Plan/Can (of beer)
Jam Jar	Car
Jellied Eel	Squeal/Deal/Feel
Jimmy Connors	Honours
Jimmy Hill	Bill/Pill
Jimmy Nail	Hell/Email/Jail
Jockey's Whips	Chips

Joe Blake	Snake/Cake/Steak
John Major	Pager/Wager
Judy Dench	Bench/Stench/Wrench
Jumbo's Trunk	Drunk
Jumpin' Jack Flash	Cash
Khyber Pass	Glass
Kidney punch	Lunch
King Lear	Ear
Kitchen Sink	Drink
Knobbly Knees	Keys
Lady in Silk	Milk
Lager and Lime	Time
Larry Flint	Skint (broke)
Laugh	Bath
Laugh and a Joke	Smoke
Lee Marvin	Starvin'
Left in the Lurch	Church
Lemon Curd	Word
Lemon Squash	Wash
Les Dennis	Tennis
Lillian Gish	Fish
Lion's lair	Chair
Little Jack Horner	Corner
Loaf of Bread	Head
London Fog	Dog
Loop the Loop	Soup
Love and Kisses	Mrs.
Lucky Locket	Pocket
Lump of Lead	Head
Macaroni Cheese	Keys

Mae West	Best
Mahatma Gandhi	Brandy/Shandy
Malcom X	Text
Marilyn Manson	Handsome
Matthew Kelly	Telly
Maurice Gibb	Fib
Michael Caine	Pain
Mickey Mouse	House
Mince Pies	Eyes
Minnie Driver	Fiver
Mork and Mindy	Windy
Mountain Ridge	Fridge
Mushy Peas	Keys
Mutt and Jeff	Deaf
Mother's ruin	Gin
Nanny Goat	Tote/Coat/Boat
Natter	Chat
Near and Far	Car/Bar
Needle and Thread	Bread
New Delhi	Belly
No Hope	Soap
North and South	Mouth
Nuns and Habits	Rabbits
Obi Wan Kenobi	Mobi (mobile phone)
Ocean Pearl	Girl
Ocean Wave	Shave
Old Joanna	Piano
Ones and Twos	Shoes
Orange and Pear	Swear
Otis Redding	Wedding

Oxford Scholar	Dollar
Oyster Bay	Gay
Pat and Mick	Sick
Peas in the Pot	Hot
Pen and Ink	Drink/Stink
Peter Pan	Old Man (father)
Piccadilly	Silly
Pie and Mash	Cash
Pig's Ear	Beer
Pins or Pin Pegs	Legs
Pitch and Toss	Boss
Plates of Meat	Feet
Pork Pies	Lies
Pots and Dishes	Wishes
Punch 'n' Judy	Moody
Queen Mum	Bum
Rat and Mouse	House
Razor	Blazer
Read and Write	Fight
Reels of Cotton	Rotten
Richard Burtons	Curtains
Richard Gere	Beer
Right Said Fred	Dead/Bread
River Nile	Denial
Rob Roy	Boy
Robin Hood	Good
Rock and Roll	Dole (welfare)
Roger Moore	Door
Roller Coaster	Toaster/Poster
Rolls Royce	Choice
Royal Navy	Gravy

Rub-A-Dub	Pub
Rubber Glove	Love
Ruby Murray	Curry
Rug Rats	Children (Brats)
Rum and Coke	Joke
Russell Crowe	Dough
Rusty Nail	Jail
Sausage and Mash	Cash/Crash
Sausage Roll	Dole (welfare)/ Goal
Scooby Doo	Clue
Sexton Blake	Fake/Steak/Cake
Skin and Blister	Sister
Sky Rocket	Pocket
Slits in a Dress	Mess
Smash and Grab	Cab
Sooty and Sweep	Sleep
Spanish Waiter	See you later
Speckled Hen	10 (£10)
Steve McQueen's	Jeans
Stevie Nicks	Flicks (movies)
Stevie Wonder	Chunder (vomit)
Sticky Toffee	Coffee
Street Fighter	Lighter
Sweaty Sock	Jock (Scottish person)
Teapot Lid	Quid/Kid
Thomas Edison	Medicine
Tick-Tock	Clock
Tiddly Wink	Drink

Tit for Tat	Hat
Tom Cruise	Booze/Bruise/ Shoes/Lose
Tom Hanks	Thanks
Tommy Tucker	Supper
Tony Blair	Hair/Chair
Trouble and Strife	Wife
Tube of Glue	Clue
Turtle Dove	Love
Turtle Doves	Gloves
Two and Six	Fix
Two-thirty	Dirty
Uncle Ben	10 (£10)
Uncle Bert	Shirt
Uncle Fred	Bread
Uncle Gus	Bus
Uncle Ned	Bed/Head
Uncle Reg	Veg (vegetable)
Uncle Toby	Mobi (cell phone)
Uncle Willy	Silly
Uncles and Aunts	Plants
Uncle Jack	Back
Vera Lynn	Gin/Chin
Veronica Lake	Brake
Vincent Price	Ice
Weeping Willow	Pillow
Westminster Abbey	Shabby
Wet and Wild	Child/Styled
Whistle and Flute	Suit
Wilson Pickett	Ticket
Wooden Pews	News

You and Me	Tea
Yogi Bear	Hair
Yul Brynner	Dinner
Zinc Pail	British Rail

There are many websites for further information about Cockney Rhyming Slang, with listings and uses of rhyming words. Here are a few:

www.cockneyrhymingslang.co.uk

www.phrases.org.uk

www.fun-with-ords.com/cockney_rhyming_slang.html

www.ruf.ride.edu/~kemmer/Words04/usage/slang-cockney.html

www.phespirit.info/cockney/

www.aldertons.com

www.peevish.co.uk/slang/articles/cockney-rhyming-slang.htm

NOTES

PRONUNCIATION GUIDE

Americans and Brits will pronounce words differently and may also spell them differently, as mentioned previously. Here are some different pronunciations:

	American	**British**
Abacus	A-ba-cus	A-BACK-us
Aluminum	alumi-NUMB	AL-lu-min-e-um
(pronunciation is different because of different spelling)		
Albino	al-bye-no	al-bean-o
Anti	aun-tie	ant-ee
Azores	A-zores	uhzores
Arctic	ardic	arc-tic
Banana	buh-nan-na	buh-NAA-na
Beta	bay-da	bee-tuh
Borough	bur-oh	bur-ah
Buoy	boo-eee	boy
Caramel	car-mul	cara-mell
Charades	sha-raids	sha-raads
Chassis	chassee	shassee
Clerk	klerk	klark
Compost	com-post	com-pahst
Consortium	con-sorsh-shum	con-sor-tee-um
Controversy	CONtro-vers-see	con-TRO-va-see
Data	day-ta	daa-ta
Due	doo	dew
Era	erra	ear-ra
Estrogen	eh-stro-gen	ee-stro-gen
Fillet	fil-lay	fil-let
Garage	garaahge	garridge
Glacier	gla sher	glacier

	American	**British**
Harem	hair-um	har-um
Herbs	erbs	herbs
Inquiries	IN-kwrees	in-KWYE-rees
Khaki	Kakky	Kah-ki
Iodine	eye-o-dine	eye-a-dean
Laboratory	lab-ra-tory	la-BOR-a-tory
Leisure	lee-shur	lez-shure
Lever	le-ver	lee-ver
Lieutenant	lu-ten-ant	lef-ten-ant
Military	military	militree
Missile	mistle	miss aisle
Privacy	pry-va-see	priv-uh-see
Progress	prog-ress	PRO-gress
Quasi	kwaz-eye	kwazee
Schedule	sked-yule	shed-yule
Semi	sem eye	sem ee
Status	stadous	stay-tus
Tomato	to-mate-toe	to-maa-toe
Urinal	your-in-al	your-I-nal
Vitamin	vy-ta-min	vi ta-min
Yogurt	yo-gurt	ya-gurt
Z	zee	zed

SPELLING DIFFERENCES

Here are just a few of the spelling differences in American English and British English:

AMERICAN	BRITISH
analog	analogue
anesthesia	anaesthesia
annex	annexe
behavior	behaviour
bylaw	byelaw
catalog	catalogue
center	centre
color	colour
criticize	criticise
curb	kerb
defence	defense
dialog	dialogue
diarrhea	diarrhoea
donut	doughnut
draft	draught
emphasize	emphasise
estrogen	oestrogen
favorite	favourite
feces	faeces
fetus	foetus
gray	grey
gynecology	gynaecology
harbor	harbour
honor	honour
humor	humour
jail	gaol

jewelry	jewellery
judgment	judgement
labor	labour
license	licence
leukemia	leukaemia
maneuver	manoeuvre
neighbor	neighbour
organization	organisation
pajamas	pyjamas
pediatric	paediatric
plow	plough
program	programme
realize	realise
skeptic	sceptic
specialty	speciality
sulfur	sulphur
tire	tyre
tons	tonnes
vice (tool)	vise (tool)

TEMPERATURE CONVERSIONS

Degrees F (Fahrenheit) to Degrees C (Celsius/Centigrade)

Take Fahrenheit temperature, subtract 32 degrees and multiply by 5/9; or take the Celsius temperature, multiply by 9/5 and add 32 degrees.

FAHRENHEIT (F)	CELSIUS (C)
104	40
98.6	37
95	35
86	30
77	25
68	20
59	15
41	5
32	0
23	-5
14	-10
5	-15
0	-18
-9	-23
-18	-28
-40	-40

NOTES

COMPARATIVE SIZES AND MEASURES

Imperial Pint	approx. 20 fluid ounces
U.S. pint	= 16 fluid ounces
Imperial Gallon	approx. 157 fluid ounces
U.S. gallon	= 128 fluid ounces
U.K. hundred weight	= 112 pounds
U.S. hundred weight	= 100 pounds

To further complicate the issue, the U.K. fluid ounce varies slightly from the U.S. fluid ounce.

The U.S. gallon = approx. 4/5 of the U.K. gallon, or the U.K. gallon is 1 ¼ times the U.S. gallon.

NOTE: In U.K. a person's weight is measured in "stones." A stone is equal to 14 pounds.

U.K. TO U.S.A. COMPARATIVE SIZES

Since clothing and shoe manufacturers vary, the comparisons made here are approximate. Generally, U.K. shoe sizes are 1 to 1 ½ sizes lower than the U.S. sizes. For example, a men's size 9 in the U.K. is about a 10 in the U.S.; a woman's size 6 U.K. is about a 7 ½ in the U.S. Women's dresses may run 2 sizes lower in the U.S. (14 U.K. is 12 U.S.). Metric sizes are also used.

ELECTRICITY   U.K. 220 volts, A.C. 50 cycles
U.S.   120 volts, 60 cycles

EMERGENCIES: U.K. dial 999   U.S. dial 911

NOTES

OTHER DIFFERENCES/CONSIDERATIONS

Traveling in either the U.S. or U.K. (or any British-influenced country) will involve more than just different words and expressions.

In U.K. you **drive on the left** - remember to "look right" when crossing the street!

Dates are written in **day/month/year** format, not **month/day/year** format as in the USA. Therefore, in Britain (and most countries of the world) 8/1/15 is **January** 1, 2015, <u>**not** August</u> 1, 2015.

Brits will include a definite article when talking about a date, such as "the ninth of September;" Americans will just say "September ninth."

Punctuation will differ, with commas and periods (full stops) being omitted/inserted in opposite ways. In U.K. addresses will include commas between numbers and street names, etc., while in the U.S. they will not. Americans will write Mr., Mrs., Dr. while British will most often write Mr, Mrs, and Dr without the period (full stop). Single quotation marks (') are often the norm in U.K. writings, as opposed to the doubles (") used in U.S. And Americans will often hyphenate words that Brits do not (first class ticket vs. first-class ticket).

Telling time: 15 minutes after the hour is called "quarter past" in British usage, "quarter after" in American usage.

The twenty-four hour clock in used in many applications (air/rail/bus timetables). For example, 1300 is 1:00 pm.

Numbers: Brits will use *nought, zero, nil,* or *oh* for sports results;American will most often use *zero* (or slang terms such as zilch or zip). In U.K. they will say "one hundred and eighty-five" while in U.S. they'll say "one hundred eighty-five" (without the "and"). Brits will use the terms double or triple/treble when numbers are repeated (i.e. "the extension is one, double five, nine" for 1559).

Brits will say **"in hospital"** while Americans will say **"in the hospital."** And **"in future"** means from now on; **"in the future"** means at some future time – Americans will say "in the future" for both meanings. When an event is postponed by rain, it's **"rained off"** in U.K. and **"rained out"** in U.S. **"Gotten"** is never used in modern British English except in expressions such as "ill-gotten gains."

American	British
"See what I bought"	"See what I've bought"
"I'll go take a shower"	"I'll go and have a shower"
"The show starts Monday"	"The show starts on Monday"
"On the weekend"	"At weekend"
"I hate math"	"I hate maths"

These are just a few of the many things you will discover different in the U.K. from the U.S.

ABOUT FOOD and DRINK...

There's a whole lot to say about the differences in the U.K. vs. the U.S. regarding food and drink. Brits will eat with both the knife and the fork, while Americans will use the knife to cut up food and then only use the fork. Lunch is usually 12 noon in U.S., 1 pm in U.K. Dinner in restaurants is often later in U.K. as well.

Iced tea is U.S. thing. Brits rarely like their tea cold, much less with ice. And on the subject of ice – cold beverages will be served with little/no ice. Beers (ales and bitters) are served warmer in U.K. – as cellar temperature retains the flavor. And mixing beer with sweet drinks is common in U.K. The legal drinking age in U.K. is 18; 21 in U.S.

An "English Breakfast," as included when staying at B&Bs normally consists of cereal, toast, eggs, sausages, bacon (more like Canadian bacon), grilled tomatoes, mushrooms, and sometimes fried bread and black pudding (blood sausage), plus tea/coffee. This is not an *everyday* breakfast for a Brit.

Tea times include "elevenses" – a morning coffee/tea break, "afternoon tea," and "high tea," which is an early evening meal (between 5 and 7 pm). If a Brit says to "call around at tea time" they usually mean to come over between 5 and 7 pm. Afternoon tea can be formal (popular in quality hotels) and include tea, jam, scones, clotted cream, sandwiches (customarily cucumber and other varieties) and possibly champagne. To further confuse you Americans call the "afternoon tea" described previously as "high tea!"

PUBS

Pubs are unique British institutions - both admirable and eccentric. They serve beer, wine, liquor, and most have "pub lunches." Children under 14 are not allowed in pubs (pubs that have gardens may allow children). Beer comes in two sizes - pints and half-pints. British beer is famous and there are stouts, porters, lagers, bitters, and ales. And it's cellar temperature - about 50 degrees (warmer than U.S.). What's on the menu? Bangers and mash (sausages and mashed potatoes), steak and kidney pie (steak and kidney in gravy baked in a pastry), fish and chips (fried fish with french fries), ploughman's lunch (ham, cheese, pickles, garnish, granary bread), prawn salad (shrimps in a mayonnaise type salad), shepherd's pie (ground beef, vegetables, and mashed potatoes cooked in a pastry), and more. Curries are popular. Starters (appetizers) or smaller meals can be "jacket potatoes" (baked potatoes filled with a variety of choices - chili, cheese, ground beef, vegetables, etc.), sausage rolls (sausages baked in pastry dough), and more. The popular meal on Sunday is roast beef/pork and gravy, yorkshire pudding (like a popover), roast and mashed potatoes with peas. A popular dessert is trifle (a mixture of sponge cake, fruit, wine, jello, custard, and cream). Stopping for a drink in the pubs is very popular. The locals have their "local," the pub they frequent. There may be darts, pool tables, and large screen TVs. Pubs are usually pleasantly decorated with bar stools, chairs or booths, lots of wood and brass, and wallpaper and carpeting that tend to give a "welcoming" look.

JUST A FEW CITIES IN U.K. AND HOW THEY ARE PRONOUNCED:

HOW DO YOU SAY...

Bournemouth	=	*Borne-muth*
Derby	=	*Darby*
Edinburgh	=	*Edin-boro*
Glasgow	=	*Glaz-go*
Gloucester	=	*Gloss-ter*
Harwich	=	*Ha-ritch*
Holyhead	=	*Holly-head*
Leicester	=	*Lester*
Luton	=	*Looten*
Norwich	=	*Norrich*
Peterborough	=	*Peter-boro*
Reading	=	*Redding*
Salisbury	=	*Sols-bury*
Slough	=	*Slou*

NOTES

U.K. - Q. & A.

Q. What is the difference between U.K. and Great Britain?

A. The U.K. (United Kingdom) is England, Scotland, Wales and Northern Ireland (or Ulster). Great Britain is Wales, Scotland, and England.

Q. Why is the U.K. such a popular destination?

A. Because of the history and scenery. It is a "heritage" place for many Americans and the language is basically the same (although this dictionary points out the differences!). The countries have a high standard of living, and transportation standards, tourist services and facilities, and health standards are very good.

Q. What kind of entertainment is there?

A. Besides restaurants, nightclubs, discos, movie heaters, shopping, theaters, and sporting events there are fairs, concerts, and tournaments, conventions, and shows.

Q. Do you have to go through customs between the countries of England, Scotland and Wales?

A. No.

Q. Is the electricity the same as the U.S.?

A. No, you will need transformers and adaptor plugs. U.K outlets are 200 - 250 volts, A.C. 50 cycles. The U.S. has 120 volt, 60 cycle electricity.

Q. *What about driving conditions?*

A. *Driving is on the left and in major cities or on the M-ways (Motorways) traffic can be really busy. In addition to driving on the left, the steering wheels of almost all cars will be on the right. If driving a stick shift car (not automatic transmission) it can make for a very confusing time at first. Roads can be narrow through small villages. Careful consideration and practice are a must. "Roundabouts" or traffic circles keep the cars moving at intersections - when approaching a roundabout slow down and yield to the traffic on the right. In towns, pedestrians have the right of way at designated crossings.*

Q. *Do I have to exchange monies?*

A. *Yes. You can exchange monies at banks, airports, train stations, post offices and change bureaus. Banks are usually the best for rates of exchange. You may also want to use a major credit card for purchases as the exchange rates for those purchases may be good. You may want to call your credit card company first to ask questions about any purchases abroad.*

BRITISH-INFLUENCED COUNTRIES

The countries listed below retain many British customs and
influence as they were or are part of the British Commonwealth.
They will have their own differences in terms and expressions
but for the most part their English will be more "British English"
than "American English."

Anguilla
Antigua and Barbuda
Bahamas
Barbados
Belize
British Virgin Islands
Cayman Islands
Guyana
Jamaica
St. Kitts
St. Lucia
Trinidad and Tobago
Turks and Caicos

In addition, countries such as India and Pakistan and many
African countries will have more British-influenced English
than American.

Australia and New Zealand have their own unique terms and
expressions although many British words are used in those
countries. Canada uses a mixture of American and British
English although spellings are primarily British.

NOTES

BRITISH HOLIDAYS AND CELEBRATIONS

U.S. legal holidays are called "bank holidays" in U.K. and there are additional "bank holidays" not celebrated in the U.S. The website www.projectbritain.com has extensive detail on British culture, traditions, festivals, and much more.

Jan. 5 – Twelfth Night – Christmas decorations need to be taken down.

Feb. 2 – Candlemas Day (Christian festival of lights)

Because the dates of the Christian festival of Lent change every year **"Shrove Tuesday"** can be in either Feb. or Mar. Shrove Tuesday (or Pancake Day) is the day before **Ash Wednesday**, and pancakes are the traditional meal.

Mar. 1ˢᵗ – St. David's Day (Wales Nat'l Day)
Mother's Day/Mothering Day is usually in March but can be in April since it occurs three weeks before Easter.
Maundy Thursday is the day before **Good Friday**, the Friday before Easter.

April 23ʳᵈ – St. George's Day (England's Nat'l Day).

May 1ˢᵗ – May Day
Early May Bank Holiday (1ˢᵗ week in May)
Spring Bank Holiday (end of May)

The Monarch's Official Birthday (sometime in June)

Late Summer Bank Holiday (end of August)

Blackpool Illuminations (begins in Sept.). The seaside town of Blackpool has 6 miles of lights and decorations)

Nov. 5 – Guy Fawkes Night (Bonfire Night) – In 1605 Guy Fawkes and a group of plotters attempted to blow up Parliament. Because the effort was thwarted the event is commemorated by fireworks, bonfires and burning effigies of "Guys."

Nov. 11 – Remembrance Day (equivalent to Veteran's Day in the U.S.) It is also known as Poppy Day because it's traditional to wear an artificial poppy.
Nov. 30th – St. Andrew's Day (Scotland's Nat'l Day).

Dec. 25th – Christmas is celebrated just as in the U.S., but **Dec. 26th** is also celebrated as **Boxing Day**. Traditionally it was the day to open the Christmas box and share the contents with the poor.

Hogmanay (Scottish) officially starts on **Dec. 31st** and New Year's Day is **Jan. 1st**
Jan. 2 - a Scottish Bank Holiday.

Note: Some companies will close for the entire week between Christmas and New Year's. **These are just some of the many holidays and celebrations.** Holidays such as Valentine's Day (Feb. 14), April Fool's Day (Apr. 1) and Halloween (Oct. 31) are celebrated in U.K. as well as the U.S.

USE THE FOLLOWING BLANK PAGES TO MAKE NOTES ON UNIQUE TERMS/EXPRESSIONS THAT YOU DISCOVER!

_____

_____

_____

_____

_____

_____

_____

_____

_____

_____

_____

_____

NOTES

THANK YOU FOR PURCHASING

The
UK to USA
Dictionary

British English vs. American English

If you would like to order copies for friends,
families, associations or any organizations
contact us:

> *Solitaire Publishing, Inc.*
> *1090 S. Chateau Pt.*
> *Inverness, FL 34450-3565*
> *(352) 726-5026*
> *e-mail: PSolitaire@aol.com*
> *www.solitairepublishing.com*

A single copy costs $9.00, including shipping
to any U.S. address. **Quantity discounts are
available.** British specialty stores and independent
bookstores may also have copies for sale/order.